Lone Star Legacy

Lone Star Legacy

The Texas Rangers Then & Now

Melanie Chrismer

PELICAN PUBLISHING
New Orleans

First printing, 2016
Second printing, 2022

Library of Congress Cataloging-in-Publication Data

Names: Chrismer, Melanie, author.
Title: Lone Star legacy : the Texas Rangers then and now / Melanie Chrismer.
Description: Gretna, Louisiana : Pelican Publishing Company, Inc., [2016] | Includes bibliographical references and index.
Identifiers: LCCN 2015050299 | ISBN 9781455621040 (pbk. : alk. paper)
Subjects: LCSH: Texas Rangers--Juvenile literature. | Law enforcement--Texas--History--Juvenile literature. | Texas--History--Juvenile literature.
Classification: LCC F391 .C486 2016 | DDC 363.2/09764--dc23 LC record available at http://lccn.loc.gov/2015050299

Printed in the United States of America
Published by Pelican Publishing
New Orleans, LA
www.pelicanpub.com

To the Texas Rangers, past, present, and future. May the Lord keep our Rangers safe, our liberty secure, and our Texas free.

For Lauren and Tim
with love

The great peace officer must have three qualities: courage, intelligence, and character. . . . Such a man cannot be scared, bought, or fooled.

Walter Prescott Webb

The Texas Rangers: A Century of Frontier Defense

Contents

Acknowledgments

With gratitude to Texas Rangers Capt. Alvin A. Alexis II, Capt. Clete Buckaloo, Capt. Bob Bullock, Lt. Jeff Collins, Jeff Cook, Joe Haralson, Capt. Howard Duane "Dino" Henderson, Lt. Brooks Long, Frank J. Malinak, Capt. Shawn Palmer, Ronald Pettigrew, Ray Ramon, Capt. Jeffery Robertson, and Lt. George Turner. Also, my thanks to Rachel Barnett, research librarian, Texas Ranger Hall of Fame and Museum (TRHFM); Christina Stopka, deputy director, TRHFM; Christina Smith, research librarian, TRHFM; Jason Walker, director of research, Texas State Cemetery; Craig Reinhold; Christine Taylor-Butler; Nina Romberg; Cynthia Leal Massey; and Judith Keeling.

Introduction

This book reviews nearly two centuries of Texas Ranger history. During that time, the state and its inhabitants went through many changes.

When discussing the people, the colony, the republic, the state, and the work of the Rangers, this book refers to the area as it was named during each time period. For example, just prior to the Republic of Texas (1836-45), the region was a part of the Mexican province of Coahuila y Tejas, and the colonies were often identified by a founder's name (Austin's Colony, et al.).

People of Texas are Texans but they also went by other names. "Texan" can be used for any era, but those who lived in the earliest Texas time were sometimes called Texicans (colonists of Mexico). By the time Texas was an independent country, the people were often called Texians. When the republic became one of the United States, most were simply called Texans. In this book, the old names are used to separate the historic time periods and identify specific circumstances.

In many cases, each American Indian group was a tribal nation unto itself. Tribesmen assisted and served with the Rangers as scouts and fighters, a part of the team.

The Texas heroes of Mexican heritage also fought for their families, homes, and territory. They are a major part of Texas history, and their sacrifices were many.

The black men who first helped in the ranks of the Rangers were sometimes compelled to do so as slaves. Over time, attitudes changed and these men were recognized too. It took longer for them, but their honorable service is remembered.

When the word *Mexican* is used in this book, it may refer to a citizen of Mexico. But at times the reference is to heritage. The terms *Hispanic Texan* and *Mexican American* are also used.

These terms are used to clearly and respectfully identify the times, places, nations, and people of Texas and its Rangers. The Texas Ranger history is a patchwork quilt of people drawn together to make a blanket of safety.

Lone Star Legacy

Texas Ranger Frontier Battalion Company D, 1887-88 (Courtesy of the Texas Ranger Hall of Fame and Museum, Waco, TX)

Chapter 1

One Legacy

A fiery horse with the speed of light, a cloud of dust, and a hearty "Hi-yo, Silver!"

Opening line from the mid-twentieth-century television series *The Lone Ranger*, starring Clayton Moore and Jay Silverheels

The Texas Rangers are a law-enforcement agency. These Texans are ready when their help is required. This organization has amazing stories and stirs up images of adventure, but these peace officers do exist. They have been active for nearly two centuries, and the facts are even more exciting than the fiction.

Movies

The Lone Ranger stories had action, the West, a sidekick, and a winning, masked hero. The television series aired in the 1950s and 1960s. Movie serials about the Lone Ranger existed in the 1940s and radio versions before that. They were favorites with fans of Westerns and generated Lone Ranger comics, lunchboxes, posters, cereals, message-decoder booklets, junior badges, and more.

These stories told great tales of justice. Best of all, the Ranger always won.

Hollywood movies about Rangers included *The Searchers* and *The Comancheros,* with actor John Wayne. The stories were set at the end of the Civil War and after. The movie *Streets of Laredo* depicted the Frontier Battalion in the late 1800s. Others featured singing cowboys, such as *Both Barrels Blazing.* Texas Rangers were portrayed as the superheroes, stealthy spies, and savvy fighters.

The problem with the movies is that they try to interpret the Ranger motivation. It is best to use facts. Rangers were, and are, much more than they have been portrayed.

Read All About It

Ranger stories helped sell newspapers in the 1800s. During the Mexican War, periodicals printed stories about the audacious, wild men of Texas.

Some incidents were true, but some of the published reports were tall tales, filled with exaggeration.

The public was hooked. Accounts handed down around campfires became seed for publication. Authors such as J. Frank Dobie, Larry McMurtry, and Elmer Kelton wrote amazing yarns, poems, and novels about the Rangers. They told of special Westerners, deadly foes, and skin-of-the-teeth escapes.

On the Small Screen

Cartoons about the Lone Ranger came along in the 1960s. Plus, there was a 1950s TV show called *Tales of the Texas Rangers*. It had a technical advisor who was a retired Ranger captain (Manuel "Lone Wolf" Gonzaullas).

Today, many remember *Walker, Texas Ranger*. This TV show had Rangers fighting updated villains in contemporary times. The characters used computer technology, modern transportation, automatic weapons, and martial arts. Hollywood keeps trying to entertain with the legacy of the Texas Rangers, but the shows are fiction, and Rangers are fact.

Sports and Parks

Some professional sports teams use the name "Rangers," complete with mascots. The New York Rangers hockey team and the Texas Rangers baseball team are two examples. Law-enforcement agencies use teamwork too, but their job is not a game.

Park rangers protect the country's natural resources, including land and animals. They, too, are not Texas Rangers.

Rangers of Old

Even the word "ranger" has a legacy. The Texas Rangers were not the first ranging minutemen. As far back as the 1400s, mounted rangers were used to protect the forests of the English kings. In King Philip's War (in the 1670s), the American colonies organized at least one ranger company to help the army.[1] Then, in the French and Indian War, the Rogers' Rangers unit was one of several gathered to assist the British army.

In the American Revolution, George Washington referred to six companies of frontiersmen as "rangers." A dozen of these units were active in the War of 1812.[2]

U.S. Army

The United States Army has maintained official units called rangers dating back to the Civil War. Those units included Terry's Texas Rangers,[3] in the Confederacy, but none of the groups were part of the Texas Rangers law-enforcement agency.

Today the U.S. Army has two battalions of an elite regiment called the Army Rangers. They are specially trained paratroopers, ready at a moment's notice to go where they are needed. These are military soldiers, not civilian crime fighters or criminal investigators. They are not, specifically, protectors of Texas, but Texas Rangers are. They have always been special citizens called to duty to serve the state of Texas.

Similar but Not

To explain the Texas Rangers' purpose, some compare them to the Federal Bureau of Investigation (FBI),[4] Royal Canadian Mounted Police (RCMPs, called "Mounties"),[5] or Scotland Yard. These are all national agencies, not state organizations. Some say the Texas Rangers are like the New Mexico Mounted Patrol, the Pennsylvania State Police, or the Georgia Bureau of Investigation (GBI). But this is not accurate either; there are many differences. The Texas Rangers have specific acceptance requirements and law-assistance and protective duties. Add to this the organization's service records (both to the Republic of Texas and the modern-day state) and length of existence, and the Texas Rangers are unparalleled.

While others are not the Texas Rangers, the word "ranger" has always represented courage.[6] The term describes a tough, brave, ready person. This unique legacy is a part of Texas history.

One Riot, One Ranger

In the 1890s, bustling cities sprang up in parts of Texas, and commerce and entertainment thrived. People were settling in, and some were making money. Laborers wanted amusements to fill their free time.

Occasionally the entertainment was illegal, such as prizefighting. Sometimes excitement, alcohol, gambling, and tempers combined to cause a riot. Local authorities protected their territories from many problems, but for bigger trouble they could send for the Rangers.

An old story tells of a city official who requested the Rangers' assistance to put down a riot. Soon a train arrived, and he met it at the station. The official anxiously awaited the men who would rescue him and save his town. All the passengers disembarked. Then one tough-looking fellow stepped from the train, with his saddle, weapon, and gear.

The nervous official looked around and asked, "Where are the other Rangers?" The man answered, "Hell! Ain't I enough? There's only one prizefight!"[7]

Most say that this man was Capt. William "Bill" McDonald. Whoever it was, the reply summed up the Rangers perfectly. The message is not bragging; it is laughing in the face of danger. It displays a confidence that anything can be accomplished. Others would later use this phrase, with their own variation. The quote has become "one riot, one Ranger!" It implies that these guys are so good they can handle any difficulty. One Ranger is enough.

In some cases, the quote has been literally true. Only one was required. On other occasions, only one was available. Some of the Rangers could be busy with other crimes or, before cars and planes, too far away to come help.

These law enforcers do work together as a team. They are not "lone rangers." One has to admire their determination and effort, as individuals and a team. They work to complete a task no matter the odds.

There have been times when more than one Ranger came to a riot. At the end of the nineteenth century, all those available were sent to El Paso to shut down the illegal gambling there. The state made its point by taking this action: even far-western El Paso must follow the law. This would apply to all

The Texas Rangers at El Paso, Texas in 1896 (Courtesy of the Texas Ranger Hall of Fame and Museum, Waco, TX)

other lawbreaking going on. The courage of one Ranger may be all that is needed to end the trouble. But every Ranger has backup.

A Part of History

Rangers have been confronting trouble since colonial Texas times. Knowing that these individuals are there is calming in itself. These people are not fictional Wild West tough guys who subdue criminals with kicks, but they are tough and simply do their job.

The group has always adapted to changing times. Everyone was expected to go where there was a need and handle whatever the difficulty was. Their accomplishments include countless investigations, innovations, victories, and arrests.

Whether working alone or as a team, Texas Rangers are ready. The facts of their service have made them legendary. What began as a necessity for survival developed into a famous institution. What started as a handful of mounted volunteers became a distinguished group of modern crime investigators. The Texas Rangers were the first state law-enforcement organization.[8] Others have since come into existence, but none are the same.

These men learned to be sharp and swift in the nineteenth, twentieth, and twenty-first centuries. They have always been a sure defense for their homeland. Through colonization, war for independence, formation of a separate republic, annexation by the United States of America, secession into the Confederate States, and eventual readmission to the U.S., the Texas Rangers have defended their territory. Through Reconstruction, industrial expansion, two world wars, the depression, technological advances, terrorism, and more, they have protected those in their care. They still do today.

How happy I am in my old age that I'm a native Texan and saw the grand frontier before it was marred by the hand of man.

Ranger James B. Gillett[9]

Chapter 2

Beginning Times

Oh pray for the Ranger, you kindhearted stranger.
He has roamed the prairies for many a year;
He has kept the Comanches from off your ranches,
And guarded your houses o'er the far frontier.

Old song mentioned in *The Mustangs*, by J. Frank Dobie

From the Start

Today, the Texas Rangers are an organization of special law-enforcement officers. They serve the state to protect the Texas laws and uphold the U.S. Constitution. They do this today and have had similar charges for nearly two centuries.

The state covers more than 268,000 square miles. That is over 171,520,000 acres. It is 879 miles from Louisiana to New Mexico. It is 888 miles from the top of the Panhandle down to the tip of the Rio Grande Valley (bordering Mexico).[1] The state has pine forests, pastures, rocky highlands, deserts, mountains, and swamps. There are river valleys, natural springs, coastal plains, sandy shorelines, farmland, and more. There is also a huge international border. Even today, with millions of people living in Texas, there are vast, wide-open spaces.

Wonders and dangers have always been present. In colonial times, there was unknown territory and almost no communication with the outside world. Eventually this big area needed a local defense.

It needed the Rangers, with their spirit of courage. It needed them to protect a land of promise—a new life and a new home.

Mexican Independence and Coahuila y Tejas

The territory now known as Texas was first owned by Spain. Then France owned it for five years, until Spain took control again in 1690. It was eventually colonized but was already inhabited by American Indians. In 1821 Mexico gained independence from Spain. Mexican colonies were established in the territory, with Empresario Stephen F. Austin as the main colony leader. An empresario was someone who was granted the right to settle on land as long as he worked to attract new settlers.

The time of peace was short. Disputes over property increased and became battles, big and small. Treaties were made and broken. Safety was a major issue, yet the Texicans were determined to stay.

In Coahuila y Tejas (the Mexican province), the United States, and Europe at that time, some people considered others as inferior.[2] Many equated their new property with their destiny. They resolved not to let anything or anyone stand in their way.

Texas was part of a Mexican province. It did not have rights like U.S. states. It was 500 miles from the Mexican capital, Mexico City, and its protection. When large problems occurred, the Texican colonists were on their own. Even if the Mexican Army came, it took a long time. The colonists themselves were the defense. That included the Rangers.

The immediate need in the area was protection from Indian attacks. This would cause Empresario Austin to call for mounted defenders. They would be minutemen who would bring their own supplies. These fighters would find their foe, perform their duty, and go back home until needed again. The men had to be focused, honorable, and ready.

Three Cultures

This territory had European and American pioneers, Mexican citizens, and at least twelve different Indian tribes.[3] The general area included all of what is now Texas and parts of New Mexico, Oklahoma, and Colorado. In the province of Coahuila y Tejas, Tejas was north of the Rio Grande (also called the Rio Bravo del Norte). This Mexican area was divided into colonies, and colonists needed permission to settle.

English, Spanish, and many American Indian languages were spoken, as well as some French and German. People knew their own language but rarely the others. However, the Mexican government demanded that all colonists speak Spanish and be Roman Catholic. The European and American colonists were predominantly Protestant and did not want to change. The Indians were not considered by the Mexican government at all. It did not think of them as colonists.

Many American Indian tribes resided in the territory before the Spaniards. By the early 1800s, Mexico took over but the Indians remained.

Some migrated as nomads over the plains and desert regions. Others were farmers in different places. Mexico decided that the tribes were not under the same colonial demands but also had no rights.

The three predominant cultures in Tejas in the 1820s (typically Anglo colonists, Mexicans, and American Indians) had different clothing, different homes, different ideas of money, and other cultural variances. The land had no unified social structure or modern communication devices.

Each culture faced harsh tests of survival. Each felt it was right and remembered what the fathers had taught. If they wanted to stay, they had to hold on to their land with everything they had. Some of the people got along, finding compromises. However, this required enormous efforts of cooperation.

There were also those who did not get along. Many tribes felt that all others, including other tribes, were invaders or potential slaves. The Mexican government allowed colonization but controlled Tejas as a wild territory. Cultures were clashing head on and trouble was all around. On all sides, people were harmed and died.

American Indians of the Territory

Life was very hard for the Texicans and from time to time there were tribal attacks. Battles were often fought over land; other times they were retaliation in order to prevent continued violence. Some of the Indians had been on the land for centuries, while other native nations had been forced to relocate there from the Eastern United States.

All of this led to bloody clashes among Indians, Anglos, and Mexicans. Tribes even fought each other. However, not every Indian was an adversary to the Texicans. Tribes would assist Texas, and its Rangers, during and after the war for independence. There would be whole American Indian Ranger units.

Today, a Texan is a Texan—no matter the heritage. In the beginning, however, heritage could separate people.

Some Indian attacks included kidnappings, and the victim's heritage was not always an issue. Indians and Mexican and Anglo colonists all saw their families ripped apart. For protection, people adopted a "shoot-first" attitude.

The Tonkawa Indians continually stole from the colony. Settler leaders confronted them and forced the chief to punish the guilty. But the Comanche posed an even bigger problem.

This was no surprise to Mexico.[4] Having colonies north of the Rio Grande was an advantage. It created a buffer between northern Mexican states and the fierce Comanche.

The Texicans also had to fend off Karankawa, who preferred eastern portions of the territory. Many of the Woodland tribes, such as the transplanted Coushatta, were considered friendly, but the Karankawa were not. Even the Spanish and French explorers recognized this. Most of the fatal encounters in the first colonial years were from Karankawa attacks. This had to stop, and Rangers would play a part in securing a treaty. Eventually the Karankawa people agreed to stay east of the San Antonio River.

The Waco and the Tawakoni tribes were very strong and violent, against other tribes as well as the settlers. They invaded Austin's Colony in 1824, hunting their enemy, the Tonkawa.[5]

In 1823, as the leader of his colony, Empresario Austin first tried diplomacy. He proposed enlisting friendly tribes as allies, but Mexico said no.[6] So he asked for volunteers to make up a rotating unit of men, providing protection at all times.

Ranging Guardians

The very first Rangers were not native Texans. They came from places such as Tennessee, Georgia, New Hampshire, as well as England. Some arrived with families, some as veterans of wars back East. This was a chance for a new life. However, they again faced threats to their safety and freedom. They fought the way they knew and learned from their new territory.

The first Rangers were called up when spies and fighting men were needed. This continued as the challenges got tougher.

A group of ranging guardians was chosen. The *milicia nacional* protected the territory under Empresario Austin's authority.[7] There were other colonies in Tejas, but this is where the Ranger history began. While large, Austin's Colony comprised only a small portion of the central area of Tejas.

Rangers such as George Erath, Jesse Billingsley, and Joseph Booth served in mounted colonial units. Early commanders were chosen by their men.

The Mexican government allowed the colonists to establish permanent settlements, which gave them legitimate Mexican authority, but Indian attacks on the colonies increased in the 1820s. The settlers were ready to fight for their new home and protect their families. A threat was there, so the Rangers had to be prepared for anything.

With the extra protection of the Rangers, Texicans continued to settle the territory. Moses Morrison, Austin Colony's second in command, endorsed using the guardians against Indian raids, and the governor of Coahuila y Tejas, José Félix Trespalacios, authorized it.[8] The defense began at the colony's boundaries. Over the next few years, the unit numbers and duties changed as needed.

From the beginning, payment was small (fifteen dollars a month, paid in land). A mounted guardian also had to supply his own horse, weapon, and food.

Weapons in the Early Days

Not every settler who came to Tejas had a rifle. It was an expense. Farmers and frontiersmen who had them used them primarily for hunting food. Protection was a secondary use. Rangers carried what they had.

A Kentucky (Sharps breech-loading carbine) was like the muskets of the American Revolution.[9] It was a muzzle-loading, single-shot rifle. Reloading took time and could not be done while riding a horse.

The Tennessee or mountain rifle was another long gun of the day. It had

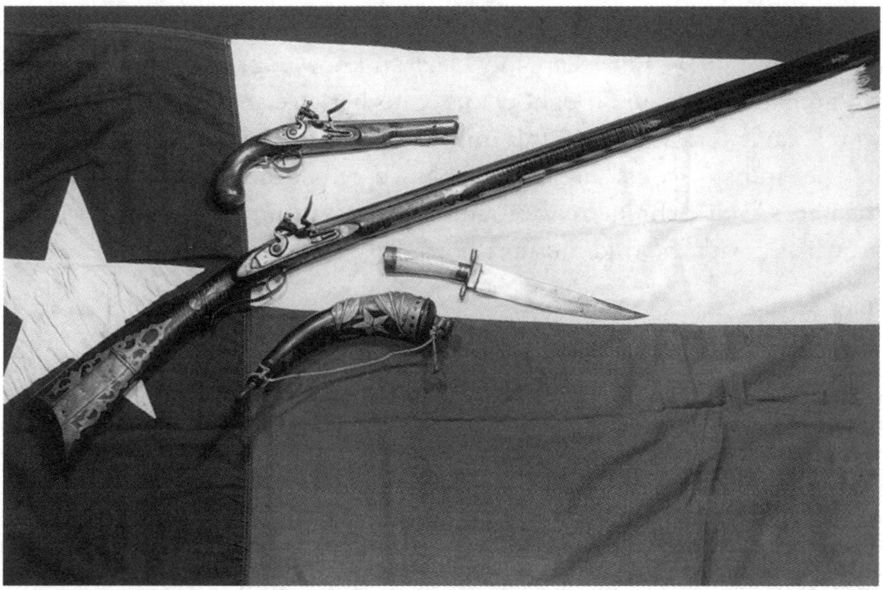

Standard weapons from the 1830s to the 1850s (Courtesy of the Texas Ranger Hall of Fame and Museum, Waco, TX)

a heavy barrel and bullets for bringing down wild animals. The sturdy stock supported the iron barrel and connecting parts. The rifle was the basic weapon by 1836. The Plains rifle (for hunting larger animals) was also popular.

These were the weapons used in the birth of the Republic of Texas. Many heroes at the Battles of Gonzales, Goliad, and the Alamo hailed from states such as Kentucky, Tennessee, and South Carolina.

The Rangers used what they knew. Eventually, their weapons were replaced with better ones.

Gun makers realized that Tejas was a good customer for their product. Every few months there would be a new weapon development. Scouting documents indicate that Ranger weapons were usually more advanced than the Mexican and American Indian ones. Tejas had direct contacts with New Jersey, Pennsylvania, Missouri, and Louisiana, which were weapon development and distribution centers. Although Tejas had the latest technology, one lost battle would give the other side the new weapon.

Later, handguns such as the Colt Dragoon, .36 caliber Colt revolvers, and a variety of Mexican pistols would also be used. Knives were standard, including the Bowie knife; special blades from Sheffield, England; crude belt knives; and butcher knives.[10]

Since Empresario Austin recruited settlers from Europe and Mexico as well as U.S. states, European and Mexican knowledge and weapons came with them. Every man brought pieces of his heritage and experience. Those who became Rangers added this information to the unit's knowledge.

The Indian scouts made valuable contributions also. Their tools, weapons, and techniques were studied. For example, Rangers became acquainted with the wild mustang horses.

The Horse

From 1823 to the 1880s, horses provided basic transportation. At first, the Rangers used their own horses brought from home, primarily Georgia, Tennessee, Virginia, and other states back East. Often they were English bred; sturdy but not built for speed. Mexican horses were generally of Spanish blood and tended to be smaller. The third type was the mustang. These equines ran wild in the West. American Indians acquired the first from the Spanish more than two hundred years before. Now they were in untamed herds. They were the fastest and the easiest to care for, used to living off the land.

1821-1844

TEXAS

1821
Mexico becomes independent nation

1823
Mexico allows establishment of colonies in Tejas

Empresario Stephen F. Austin calls for organization of "rangers"

1833
Antonio López de Santa Anna becomes dictator of Mexico

1836
March 2, Texas declares independence from Mexico; the Alamo

April 21, Texas wins independence from Mexico (Battle of San Jacinto)

1840
Council House Fight

UNITED STATES

1821
California becomes part of Mexico

1823
The Monroe Doctrine

1830
U.S. Congress passes Indian Removal Act

1838
Samuel Morse sends first message using his code taps

1844
James Polk elected 11th U.S. president

THE WORLD

1821
English scientist discovers properties of electromagnetism

1831
Victor Hugo publishes, *The Hunchback of Notre-Dame*

1835
Halley's Comet

1837
Victoria becomes queen of England

Texas History

Texas history and the Texas Rangers cannot be separated. They are a part of each other. Both the colonies and the Comanche were determined to stay. As the colonies faced a continuing threat, Rangers were on the job.

Employ ten men . . . to act as rangers for the common defense.

Empresario Stephen F. Austin requesting two companies of Rangers for the protection of Austin's Colony[11]

Chapter 3

The War for Independence

Remember the Alamo, remember Goliad!
Texians at San Jacinto, 1836

Change Was Coming

Military units have their own flag or guidon for identification. In times past, the flag was taken into battle. If the flagbearer was wounded or killed, another soldier would pick it up and carry it forward. Each Texas era has produced Texas Rangers who picked up the guidon. This was especially true when Texas declared independence.

When Indian attacks increased, Texas Rangers had to protect on the move. The units began scouting for trouble, looking for evidence of activity. Soon parties were scouting for signs of the Mexican Army, too. The independent spirit of Texas was about to declare itself.

By 1835, tensions between the Texicans and the Mexican government were becoming clear. The Texicans were dealing continually with Indian attacks, and Mexico was not helping. Freedom of religion and other rights were not available to them. Settlers remembered certain liberties they used to have in the U.S.

Less than sixty years had passed since a war was fought with England over similar issues. The taste of unalienable rights was still in the Texicans' mouths. They hungered for it again.

The Mexican government began to suspect problems and conspiracies. Several years earlier, Mexico sent inspectors and spies to report on the northern situation. The government wanted to know if the settlers were speaking Spanish, complying with the ban on slavery, and honoring the mandate to join the Catholic Church. The spies reported that many of these orders were being ignored. So in 1830, Mexico refused to let any more colonists into Texas. This did not stop the settlers from coming, however.

This law reminded Texicans of past tyrannies in their history. In the fall of 1835, leaders of the colony gathered. They created a representing body called the Permanent Council.

Corps for Protection

War seemed inevitable, so an army would be needed. For now, the council relied on what they knew. In October 1835, they resolved to form a "Corps of Rangers,"[1] which would consist of "twenty-five rangers to range and guard the frontiers between the Brazos and Trinity rivers."[2] By November, the area was expanded to between the Colorado and Guadalupe rivers. This would mark the official formation of the Texas Rangers. The commanders in this first corps were called superintendents.[3]

The corps had three companies, each with a captain and lieutenants. Again, each man brought a good horse, saddle, bridle, blanket, and 100 rounds of powder and ball for his muzzle-loading rifle. They were each paid $1.25 a day for their rations, clothing, and horse upkeep.

The captains of these companies were William H. Arrington, Isaac W. Burton, and John J. Tumlinson. Maj. Robert M. "Three-Legged Willie" Williamson was elected as the commander of the entire corps. Major Williamson suffered an illness as a child that left him with a permanently bent leg, but this did not stop him from leading the Rangers. He used a peg leg to walk.[4]

Williamson was born in Georgia, in 1806. At twenty-one, he came to Texas. He was a delegate to the Texas Convention of 1833 and called the "Patrick Henry of the Texas Revolution."

Comanche at Walnut Creek

In January of 1836, the three Ranger companies (fifty-six men each) covered the region. With Texas seeking independence, the colonists would need protection from Mexico. Simultaneously, tribal attacks increased now that the settlers were distracted with war preparations.

Ranger Noah Smithwick (under Capt. John J. Tumlinson) recorded a rescue. At Hornsby's Station (near present-day Austin), his company saw a tired and bleeding woman stagger toward them. Eventually she was able to tell her story.

Comanche attacked her family as they traveled from the Guadalupe River. Her husband and brother were killed, and she and her two children were taken captive. The Indians killed her daughter but her son survived.

While they were on the move, the weather turned cold. The captors made camp to wait out the storm, and everyone wrapped themselves up in buffalo skins. The Comanche trusted her not leave her son.

She waited until everyone was asleep, then escaped to get help. She followed a stream, which led her to some cows. She stayed with them, hoping they belonged to settlers.

The Texas Rangers went to save the boy. The next morning, Captain Tumlinson, his men, and scouts found the Comanche trail at Walnut Creek and surprised the Indians. They fought hand to hand. The Rangers rescued the boy and brought him back to his mother.[5]

Gonzales, the Alamo, and Goliad

By this time, separation from Mexico was sure. Soon the fighting would be bloody. First there was Battle of Gonzales.

Mexico knew that Texas was seeking independence, so they started to secure their authority. They demanded that the cannon in Gonzales be returned. It had been provided for colonial security. The Texicans interpreted this demand as a sign that Mexico wanted them defenseless. No longer feeling any loyalty, they sent a message back. It said, "Come and take it!" Those words were put on a flag and raised at Gonzales.

The cannon stayed. On February 3, 1836, Col. William B. Travis and his men joined others at the Alamo in San Antonio. This would be their headquarters and the fortification of defense for their statement of freedom. Travis called for men to help defend the Alamo. Mexican general Antonio López de Santa Anna and his soldiers were marching north. In all, General Santa Anna had close to 5,000 men. There were around 190 Alamo defenders.

On March 2, Texas officially declared its independence. But the siege of the Alamo had already begun. The settlers no longer thought of themselves as Mexican colonists. They were separate. They were Texians.

The message of independence spread from town to town. The garrison desperately needed reinforcements. The thirty-two Gonzales Rangers answered the call, but they were the only ones. By March 6, all of the Alamo defenders were killed. The Gonzales Rangers are honored today as the Immortal Thirty-Two.

The Battle of the Alamo was devastating. Brave men died, seeing no mercy. It was now independence from Mexico or nothing.

Three weeks later, on Palm Sunday, the pattern of Santa Anna's brutality was repeated. This time, more lives were lost. When Texians at the Goliad Mission heard about the Alamo, they surrendered. All the same, approximately 350 men were marched into a field and shot. If any Texians were not ready to be separate before, Goliad changed their minds. Now the issue was to save their families. The Mexican Army was marching north, and this started the Runaway Scrape.

The Runaway Scrape

The Runaway Scrape was a scene of fear, urgency, anger, and desperation. It was life or death for the Texians. The fastest transportation was horse or wagon. A family had to fit everything and everyone into one wagon pulled by a horse or ox. It was called the Runaway Scrape because it was like scraping up a hill to get away from a flood.

Some did not want the Mexicans to have what was left behind. So they set fire to their leavings. Texas Rangers protected the families as they fled north and east to the U.S.

Noah Smithwick was again one of guardians. Under the direction of Major Williamson, Smithwick and other Rangers stayed behind, looking for the Mexican Army. They sank boats that might assist the enemy and tried to rescue cattle. When these Rangers finally caught up to the Runaway Scrape trail, they found whole towns empty. Doors were left open; breakfast was on tables; livestock wandered free.

One of the Rangers was Erastus "Deaf" Smith. He scouted the area and provided defense for the fleeing settlers. He is famous for making sure that Texians got across a bridge and then burning it before the Mexican soldiers could use it.

Battle of San Jacinto

The Mexican Army went east, then north. Its battle with Gen. Sam Houston's army would decide the fate of Texas. It was fought at San Jacinto, near present-day Houston, on April 21, 1836. Some Rangers fought in the Texas Army, while other units continued to guard the Runaway Scrape.

The Texians won their independence. Their sacrifice allowed the region to become a separate nation, the Republic of Texas.

"Remember the Alamo, remember Goliad" was the call from then on. The most hated man, above all others, was Santa Anna. Once he was back in Mexico, he disregarded the treaties he signed at San Jacinto and ended the promised cooperation. Mexico tried to reacquire Texas (or portions of it) for decades, which led to more deaths. Distrust on both sides of the border and further invasions resulted in ill-fated fights. One attempted Mexican invasion was by sea.

The Horse Marines

Ranger Capt. Isaac Burton had thirty men to patrol the Gulf Coast regions for signs of Mexican attack. On June 3, they spotted a ship in Copano Bay (between present-day Rockport and Refugio). Burton's men lured it into sending a boat ashore. After capturing five Mexicans, sixteen of Captain Burton's company rowed back to the ship and captured it also. The Mexican vessel, its crew, and all its supplies were now under Texian control. The ship was bringing provisions to the Mexican Army for a potential invasion.

Then two other Mexican vessels anchored off a nearby sandbar. The Rangers captured these captains as well. Now Texas had three ships and $25,000 worth of supplies.

Burton's Rangers turned everything over to the Texas Army. They had taken on new challenges and were now ranging the waves. This earned the company the title of the Horse Marines.[6]

So, the government provided their protection as best it could with the means at its disposal, graciously permitting the citizens to protect themselves by organizing . . . ranging companies.

Ranger Noah Smithwick [7]

Chapter 4
The Republic

I will not fight Jack Hays anymore for he has a shot for every finger on his hand.

American Indian speaking about Ranger Capt. John Coffee Hays and the five-shot Colt Paterson revolver

A Separate Nation

From 1836 to 1845, the Republic of Texas was a separate nation. Most of the land was not mapped yet. It was no longer part of Mexico and not yet part of the U.S., but its heritage was predominantly Mexican. The Mexican, Anglo, and all other residents were Texians now. There was a new set of circumstances for them and the Indians as well.

What happened next would depend on who was the president. Every new administration established new policies toward Mexico, the native tribes, the U.S., and the Texas Rangers. Each president called upon the Rangers and made changes to the organization, such as how to use them, strategies relating to the Indians, and methods of payment. The new Republic had limited funds to run a country, and payment for Ranger service was slow or nonexistent. Many big plans were never implemented.

David Burnet was the first president of Texas. He served from the time independence was declared to the actual victory over Mexico. Pres. Sam Houston (the general of the Battle of San Jacinto) was the first and the third president of the Republic. His decisions and actions were very different from those of the next president, Mirabeau Lamar. The final president, Anson Jones, served until Texas joined the U.S.

President Houston encouraged friendship and cooperation with the American Indians and opposed slavery. He favored putting the war with Mexico in the past, so he reduced the military to a minimum.

The Texas Congress disagreed and passed a law obligating the president to "protect the frontier." Specifically, this included defense against hostile Indians. This law kept ranging units functioning. The mounted men were ready to go wherever they were needed, but this time they were Rangers for their own nation.

Help from American Indians

The same law provided for help from friendly Indian scouts. These men served with the Anglo and Mexican Rangers, and most knew some English. A lot of the native Rangers were from the Tonkawa and Keechi tribes. They had a common enemy—the Comanche., including Tonkawa scouts Placido and Antonio. By 1839 there were at least two Indian ranging companies. Lipan chiefs Castro and Flacco were helpful allies against the Comanche. They worked closely with Capt. Jack Hays.

Tribes and individuals made choices for or against the new Texas, and the choices were not always easy. In 1839, Texas Cherokee chief Bowles told peace-treaty commissioners, "If I fight, the whites will kill me. If I refuse to fight, my own people will kill me." He chose his people, and he died fighting against the Anglos.[1]

Tug-of-War Politics

While President Houston had pursued peace with the native peoples, President Lamar's plan was to remove them from the region. He wanted to expand the settled areas, strengthen the regular army, and use the Rangers to protect it.

President Lamar then moved the capital to Austin. This community was on the very edge of Comancheria (the land of the Comanche).[2]

The Council House Fight

In 1840 a terrible incident increased Anglo-Indian bitterness. In January, after numerous Comanche attacks and swift retaliatory raids, three Comanche chiefs asked for a conference. Because Henry Wax Karnes had once been their captive, he knew the Comanche ways. They asked to talk to the "red-headed ranger."[3]

Ranger Karnes communicated with the Comanche, who told him they wanted peace. He informed them that they would have to return all their captives. Twenty days later, the Comanche came to the San Antonio council house (or courthouse) to meet with Texian envoys. At that time Karnes was in New Orleans, not San Antonio.

The March 19 conference between the chiefs and Texian emissaries (the Texas secretary of war, Gen. A. S. Johnston, and three army units) turned deadly. By the end of the day, forty-two people lost their lives. Thirty-five were Comanche, including chiefs, three women, and two children. Seven Texians were killed and ten injured. After the fight, the army took twenty-

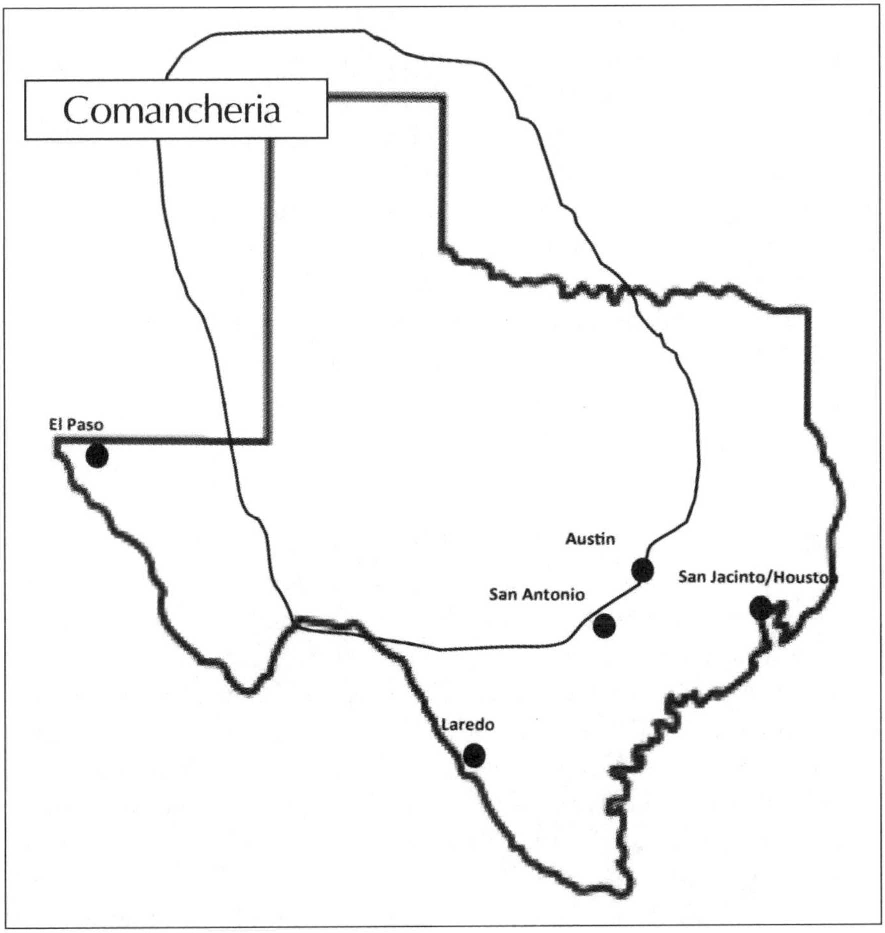

Approximate area of Comancheria, the land of the Comanche

seven Comanche women and children captive. This was called The Council House Fight.

It was not a Texas Ranger encounter. But it affected them, because they had to fight more battles with the Comanche. After the Council House Fight, distrust grew on both sides. The Comanche and the Texians were bitter enemies, fighting over the same land. Fierce clashes continued, and the Republic's Rangers were the Indian-fighting experts.[4]

Rangers for the Republic

In the Republic years, captains such as Isaac Burton, John Tumlinson, and Jack Hays were inspirations. When fighting Indians, Tumlinson found that he should never underestimate the enemy. Others realized that not all Indians were the enemy.

Capt. J. R. Cunningham demanded honor in his men. Once when a Ranger looted, Captain Cunningham gave discipline through humiliation. They were there to fight and protect, not treasure hunt. The thief's shirt was torn from "his back and [his] arms painted [and] his head covered with a red flannel cap, with flowers." Then he had to ride backward on a tailless mule through the middle of San Antonio, with the rest of the unit marching silently behind him. Afterward, the man left in disgrace.[5]

Texas Rangers are human and make mistakes. By and large, their mistakes are few and subsequently corrected.

Plum Creek

Following the Council House Fight, a captured Indian woman was sent to the Comanche to deliver an ultimatum. They were to release their hostages or else. The reply was not what Texas wanted. The answer came in violence against the Republic.

In August 1840, a large war party of twenty-seven attacked the Lavaca settlement (present-day Port Lavaca). One man was killed and another wounded. By August 7, twenty-two Lavaca men joined Capt. Mathew "Old Paint" Caldwell and his thirty-seven Gonzales Rangers. The next morning, a large Comanche party struck the coastal community of Linnville. The settlers escaped into the nearby bay.

The attack went on all day, with looting, burning, and widespread destruction. Horses were taken and other animals slaughtered. Five Linnville men were killed. At the end the day, the attackers left with mounds of stolen goods. They also had captives: two women and a child. The Indians headed west on one of their regular paths, with Rangers and militia on the trail.[6]

The day after this attack, Captain Tumlinson's group found the Comanche. One Texian was killed, but the real battle would take place a few days later. By August 10, Captain Caldwell's group reached Seguin, Texas. He decided to confront the Comanche at Plum Creek (southeast of Austin).

More men joined Caldwell and the militia, including some army regulars. Col. Edward Burleson came with 100 men. This included Placido and 13 Tonkawa Rangers. The Tonkawa tribe wanted to live in safety from the Comanche also.[7]

Surprise now seemed to be on the Texians' side. When they caught up to the Comanche on August 12, it was not just a band of warriors but women and children, too. On top of that, there were captive people, large bundles of stolen goods, and a tremendous herd of horses.[8]

When the native leaders spotted the Texians, they attempted to distract their enemy. They rode their horses ahead and steered the herd into the Texian path. The chief rode in the open and was shot.

The Texian charge was met by stampeding horses and galloping Comanche warriors decorated with their Linnville plunder. It was a terrible battle, with Comanche bodies scattered all around Plum Creek. All but one of the captives, from Linnville and Victoria, Texas, were returned alive.

Small groups of warriors would still fight bloody battles from time to time. However, this was one of the last large Comanche fights with Texas. They never again ventured that deep into the well-settled territory. Plum Creek was a turning point for both sides.

Obstacles for the Force

Texas Rangers fought off violent attacks from tribes and unconventional warfare from Mexican bandits. They also helped repel further Mexican invasions. Many of those who fought for Texas independence in the regular ranks were now serving in mounted rifle companies.

Antonio Menchaca, Lewis Sánchez, and Jose Maria Gonzales were some of the important Texas Rangers of Mexican ancestry. In the early days of the Republic, they served in Mexican or mixed Anglo-Mexican units.[9] Like the Indian scouts, those of Mexican heritage faced some obstacles.

The Republic of Texas demanded full loyalty, as did Mexico. Each man had to make a choice. Some of the Hispanic patriots who fought for Texan independence eventually decided to return to Mexico. This caused resentment among the Texians, and the numbers of Mexican Rangers declined.

Capt. Jack Hays

In the Republic days, the men mostly served in smaller units in their home counties.[10] They defended that territory. Rangers used their frontier experiences as training, but that training would change when one of the most respected and successful commanders came to the forefront. That man was Ranger Capt. Jack Hays.

Capt. John Coffee Hays (Courtesy of the University of Texas at San Antonio Libraries Special Collections)

Jack Hays was born in Tennessee and came to Texas in 1836. His father had served with both Andrew Jackson and Sam Houston. When Hays arrived, he had a letter of recommendation addressed to the Texas president.

Most of Texas was uncharted land and needed to be measured and mapped. The new Texian learned to be a surveyor and went to work around San Antonio. He was also a Ranger scout. Hays assisted Henry Karnes, Sam Maverick, and Juan Seguín on expeditions. He became an experienced scout, spy, and Ranger. He became a captain and was respected both by his men and his enemies.

By 1840, Texas was basically at war with the Comanche. Captain Hays realized that his men would have to fight like Comanche in order to beat them. He observed the enemy, and using the native warriors' fighting techniques, he improved his unit's ability. Hays prepared them with training sessions.[11] Then, when the time came, he led them in battle and gave credit to any brave man.

Training

The Texas Rangers had to learn how to properly use their supplies, including weapons. They did not want to waste anything—food, horses, ammunition, effort, or a good man. Capt. Jack Hays made sure his men knew how to fight on the range.

Hays Rangers trained with both rifles (such as the Kentucky) and Colt pistols. Shooting came naturally to them, as many had grown up using rifles. And the enemy did not have multi-shot pistols.

They set up targets and fired their weapons over and over again. Wooden stakes and other targets had no chance as the men practiced both at a gallop and standing still. A member of Hays' unit was expected to shoot, then duck down and load any gun. He had to do this while riding a horse.

The Rangers also practiced Indian and Mexican horsemanship. Both groups were superior riders. First, the horses had to be fed correctly. Then they had to be used well in quick-hitting, surprise battles. The grain-fed horses had more energy and ran faster than horses that just ate hay.

Hays was an innovator. He had his men switch to a heavier Spanish bit. Now they could control their horses with one hand. This meant that a rider could hold a weapon when riding fast in a fight.

Hays had his men learn what to do if they dropped their gun. They practiced slipping down on one side of the horse, just like the Comanche. The natives were famous for this. Hays wanted his men to be able to do anything the Comanche could. Trick-riding Rangers could pick up weapons in the middle of a battle. By the end of that first training session, they could even pick up a coin.

There is an old saying about these Rangers. They could "ride like Mexicans, trail like Indians, shoot like Tennesseans, and fight like the devil."[12] This was a great compliment, because Mexicans were the best horsemen, Indians were the finest scouts, Tennessee frontiersmen were known for their long-rifle accuracy, and Texas Rangers were renowned for their fighting ability.

The Rangers learned to be prepared for anything. They became experts at quickly switching from trail scouting to full fighting. It was life or death.

Hays taught the men to wait for the right time to attack. He learned this from watching his foes. Mexican army units and the Comanche would lure their enemies into ambush. With training, Rangers could apply these learned skills and survive. Practiced readiness got the job done.

Having the Edge

In 1836, Rangers used one-shot, muzzle-loading rifles or one-shot pistols. Since that rifle could not be reloaded on horseback, they had to stop, dismount, reload (with both hands), and then shoot again. Many arrows could be shot at the Rangers in the time it took them to make one, muzzle-loading shot. They needed a better, faster weapon. Thanks to weapons inventor Samuel Colt, the Texas Rangers got the repeating revolver.

The U.S. government bought Colt's pistols for military use but not as many as he had hoped. When the Republic of Texas saw the weapon's potential, things changed. The Lone Star State was Colt's first big customer. The weapon was called the Texas Colt.

The new five-shot Colt Paterson revolver was the answer for the Rangers.[13] An accurate shot from a handgun could prevent a deadly lance or arrow attack. Still, the gun was not perfect. It was extremely hard to reload on a horse, and if any gun part broke, it could be fatal for the user.

To find an answer to these problems, Ranger Samuel Walker was sent to Paterson, New Jersey to meet with Samuel Colt in 1846. Walker, originally from Maryland, met Colt at Samuel Hall's gun store. The three Sams got together and reinvented the weapon, resulting in the Colt Walker. The upgrade had a heavier frame and was now .44 calibers. The grip was balanced and shaped for ease of use, and now the gun was a six-shooter.

The redesign fit specifications described by the Texas Rangers. The men would no longer need to dismount to reload. Until then, enemies of Texas often had the edge.

Battle of Walker's Creek

In 1844, Captain Hays and his men scouted between the Pedernales and Llano rivers. President Houston was in the middle of negotiations with tribal leaders, and one tribe was causing problems. Hays' job was to investigate and

Colt Walker revolver, the weapon that gave the Texas Rangers the edge over their enemies (Courtesy of the Texas Ranger Hall of Fame and Museum, Waco, TX)

identify the reason. He followed his instructions exactly.[14] On the way back, the Rangers camped at what was later called Walker's Creek.

Captain Hays was always alert. He put four men farther back from the unit to cover the rear. These Rangers spotted a group of Comanche, Waco, and Mexicans, so they galloped up and alerted the camp. Hays reported, "I immediately ordered my men to saddle, and prepare to fight; for I could have no doubt but that their intentions were hostile."[15]

They did not rush the attackers. Instead, they waited. Experience told them this was the way to save lives. There were only fifteen Rangers, and the assailants might outnumber them.

When the attackers saw them, they circled around the Rangers and tried to get them to chase them. Captain Hays rejected the bait and kept his men at a walk. Finally, the native warriors gave up and rode away.

Suddenly, more tribesmen appeared at the top of a nearby hill. There were almost seventy on horseback with lances and shields. They yelled down, taunting their enemy. But the Rangers did not waste their ammunition. Hays' experience made him order his men to hold their ground. He was there to gather information for his president. He did not want a battle unless it was necessary.

Each side was changing the rules of engagement, using knowledge of the other to fight better. They were learning how to beat their enemy. For those at Walker's Creek, the negotiations were over.

Fighting on wooded hills is different from combat in an open field. Hays used this to his advantage. At the base of the hillside, the Texas Rangers were hidden. Some of the attackers rode down for a better look. In the meantime, the Ranger captain ordered his men around and up the hill for a surprise attack. By the time the Indians realized the maneuver, Texian guns were shooting at them. Several ponies lost their riders, and Rangers chased the braves down the hill to flat ground. Hays' men were still outnumbered.

The attackers planned to ambush the Rangers and fight them hand to hand. They were expecting only one Texian bullet at a time. Instead, the outnumbered defenders fired five shots at a time without any reloading. The five-shot Colt revolver and Hays' coolheaded tactics won the day. The surviving attackers left as quickly as they could, but the battle was not over.

At least two of Hays' men were separated from the rest. The assailants regrouped and ferociously attacked Samuel Walker and R. A. Gillespie. These men were lanced but survived. W. B. Lee and Andrew Erskine were also injured but kept fighting. Ranger Peter Fohr was killed. Some of the men were able to reload and had five new shots ready to go. Even Ranger Gillespie reloaded his rifle. Hays knew that his unit might not survive another attack. The way to stop the fight was to kill the chief. Gillespie was the one with a reloaded rifle. He took the shot and the battle was over.

The Indian group left the field quickly. The Rangers were in no shape to pursue. After a day of rest, they headed back to headquarters.

Training and upgraded weaponry helped the Rangers win the Battle of Walker's Creek. They would also pay off in battles to come. This was another turning point. Hays gave credit to the "five-shooting pistols."[16] These guns gave them offensive abilities against skillful and numerous foes. As always, Hays commended his men. He was a great leader, and part of that came from his respect for those who served with him.

The enemy saw the difference also. Hays showed the advantage of strength, readiness, knowledge of the enemy, and the latest technology. Hays established a foundation for future Texas Rangers.

Man who it is very bad luck to get into a fight with because devils side with him.

Comanche name given to Ranger Capt. Jack Hays[17]

Chapter 5

Mexican Invasions Continue

The enemy are all around me on every side; but I fear them not. . . . There are eleven hundred of the enemy. I can whip them on my own ground without any help, but I cannot take prisoners.

Mathew "Old Paint" Caldwell, commander of the Texas forces, calling for reinforcements against Mexican Gen. Adrián Woll at the Battle of Salado Creek, 1842

Santa Anna Tries Again

Early in 1842, President Santa Anna sent Gen. Rafael Vasquez and 500 soldiers north to Texas.[1] Mexico had invaded again, attacking San Antonio and two other cities.

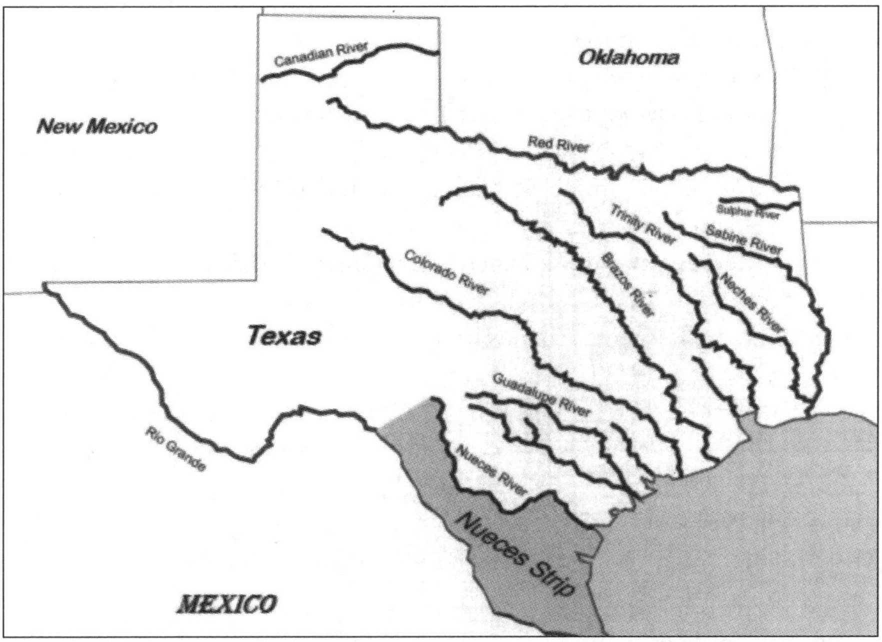

The Nueces Strip, at times claimed by Texas (and then the U.S.) and Mexico (Courtesy of WMC)

Mexico had never accepted the Rio Grande as the international border. They considered the border to be the Nueces River (farther north). This put in dispute anything south of an invisible line from Corpus Christi to Del Rio (and farther west into Big Bend). This area was called the Nueces Strip.[2]

The Mexicans held San Antonio for two days. Then they retreated back to the border with Rangers on the trail. By the summer, Mexico invaded once more. Santa Anna sent about 1,500 men back to San Antonio, led by Gen. Adrián Woll. This was three times as many soldiers, armed Mexican citizens, cavalry, and cannons as before. They would face only 200 Texas Army soldiers, Texas Rangers, and untrained volunteers.

General Woll

On September 11, 1842, San Antonio woke up to a cannon blast. General Woll had captured the city and fifty-three Texians. He declared Texas to be reconquered.

Captain Hays wrote a letter to the citizens of Texas. He knew the Mexican soldier fighting techniques and that only a strong resistance could restore peace. Hays called for assistance. He warned that another wave of Mexican soldiers was surely coming.

The Texians gathered volunteers for a week. Strategies were planned as Captain Hays' group continued to spy on the Mexican troops. The deciding fight was the Battle of Salado Creek, a place of Texian choosing. The Mexican Army, approximately 40 Cherokee, and 100 San Antonians fought against the Texas forces.

When Mexico invaded, Ranger "Old Paint" Caldwell was appointed commander of the Texas forces.[3] Called the "Paul Revere of the Texas Revolution," he was a courageous, flamboyant man with white splotches in his hair.

At that time, Salado Creek was more like a river. This prevented the Mexican forces from attacking on many sides. Before the battle, Colonel Caldwell asked Ranger Zachariah Morrell, a pastor, to speak to the men.[4] Many Texians had already died, and it was time to fight and fight hard. The Baptist minister told the men to shoot low and aim first for those with swords and officers' hats.

During the battle, some Texians were cut off from the larger group. They fought as long as they could but finally tried to surrender. However, they were shot. Eventually, Caldwell had to call for reinforcements.

The Mexican Army had heavy losses too and retreated toward Mexico. The invaders took prisoners, however, including some Rangers. The other Texians chased the Mexican Army for several days. They experienced bad weather and lack of both sleep and food. Families were left unguarded at home. This changed the minds of some of the pursuing Texians. The men were divided over whether to rescue the captives or consider the invasion finished and go home.

General Woll returned to his country with about two hundred former Texians now siding with Mexico. This included former Ranger Captain Antonio Perez, who joined Woll's army.

Many Texians of Mexican descent, such as Ranger Antonio Coy, stayed with Texas, especially in San Antonio. They made a choice, and this was their home. Coy and Antonio Menchaca continued to be Rangers.

The Mier Expedition

The Texas defense force never caught up with the Mexican retreat. But plans were made to try again to follow Woll into Mexico. Brig. Gen. Alexander Somervell divided the men into two groups. One was a spying unit under Capt. Jack Hays, and the rest were soldiers led by Capt. Samuel Bogart. However, the groups did not work well together.

Hays' unit included several Rangers, and they followed his orders. Not everyone knew it, but President Houston had also given Hays separate orders. He was to watch over Bexar County (around San Antonio). He had to protect the county, train his men, supply them, and recruit while maneuvering to the border.

New recruits had no experience. Young farmers saw the expedition as an adventure, not a dangerous military campaign. This made the units careless and weak. They were careless with campfires and allowed a Mexican prisoner to escape.

By the time the Texians reached Laredo, they had 200 fewer men than when they started. They took the town, and some looted it. This was not their purpose. Military discipline was falling apart.

General Somervell called off the expedition, but some of his army disobeyed and headed to Ciudad Mier, across the Rio Grande. Captain Hays and Ranger Benjamin H. McCulloch returned to their regular responsibilities, in Texas.

A few of Hays' men continued into Mexico and participated in what was called the Mier Expedition.[5] Samuel Walker, William A. A. "Big Foot" Wallace, John McMullen, and James L. Truehart fought at Mier and were captured. Rangers William Eastland and Ewen Cameron, while serving in Somervell's regular army, were also captured. The captives were marched farther into Mexico as prisoners of war.

Black Bean Incident

On the way to Mexico City, the Texians attempted an escape. But in the desolate areas of Northern Mexico, most died or were recaptured. A small group of the escapees did make it back to Texas.[6] Ranger Nelson Lee was one of them.[7]

During the escape, five Mexican soldiers were killed. Mexico ordered one out of every ten captured Texians executed. The condemned were chosen by chance. Those who drew a white bean from an earthen jar lived. Those who drew a black one died.

William Eastland drew a black bean. Ewen Cameron drew a white one but was executed anyway. Mexican commanders thought he was the instigator of the escape. Ranger Joe Berry also died during the Mexican imprisonment.

Those who went to Ciudad Mier made their choice as independent citizens. The Black Bean Incident survivors suffered for nearly two years in the Mexican prisons. Only some made it home.

The qualities necessary in a genuine ranger were a fleet horse, an eye that could detect the trail, a power of endurance that defied fatigue, and the faculty of looking through the double sights of his rifle with a steady arm.

Nelson Lee, Texas Ranger[8]

Chapter 6

Republic Law Becomes State Law

[Hays'] Rangers have come, their appearance never to be forgotten. Not any sort of uniforms, but well mounted and doubly well armed: each man has one or two Colt's revolvers besides ordinary pistols, a sword, and every man a rifle. . . . The Mexicans are terribly afraid of them.

Gen. Ethan Allen Hitchcock, U.S. Army, during the Mexican War

The Twenty-Eighth State

In 1845, the U.S. flag got a new star when Texas became the twenty-eighth state. Texas's hope was to hand their frontier problems (Indians and Mexico) over to the federal government. Texas officials also thought American statehood might remove their treasury burdens.

The U.S. acquired Texas entirely—all of its bills and fights. But Texas still had to do its part.

The Texans (now U.S. citizens) were sure they knew best how to do their fighting and set their policies. But the U.S. government was the authority now. It sent army units for internal and external protection. Washington applied its own rules, and Texas was not used to this.

The state now had to ask the U.S. government to pay for essentials. Permission was required, and so was a lot of paperwork. The Lone Star State was now just one of many. Its major problems would be handled just like those of all the other states. The U.S. Army and U.S. Indian agents would deal with tribal troubles.

U.S. policies frustrated the independent Texans. Texas Indians often found them confusing, also. The policies were supposed to protect everyone. The U.S. demanded that the Comanche and Apache stop raiding Mexico. Texas never suggested or worried about this before. But from this point on, it was a rule. The statehood star gave Texas many advantages, but it also brought dissatisfaction.

1845-1885

TEXAS

1845
Texas becomes 28th state

1847
Colt Walker revolvers arrive for U.S. troops in Mexican War

1861
Texas secedes from Union

1870
Texas accepted back into Union

1874
Texas Ranger divisions, Frontier Battalion and Texas Ranger Force, organized

UNITED STATES

1845
John Tyler, 10th president, sets first uniform Election Day

1846
The Mexican War

1861
The Civil War begins

1865
Gen. Lee surrenders to Gen. Grant

Abraham Lincoln, 16th president, assassinated

Reconstruction begins

1876
Alexander Graham Bell gets patent for the telephone

THE WORLD

1845
Irish Potato Famine

1847
Charlotte Bronte's novel *Jane Eyre* published

1865
Gregor Mendel discovers principles of genetics

1883
Volcano Krakatoa erupts in Pacific Ocean

1885
Gottlieb Daimler invents and patents motorcycle

The Mexican War

Only a year after Texas's statehood, war broke out between the United States and Mexico. It was the beginning of a new experience for the U.S. Army—and a chance for Texas to get even. They were fighting Mexico again and they knew how to do that. The Texans had a reputation for being fierce and effective fighters. They were unsurpassed in their knowledge of the area and enemy. Their reputation would only increase.

At times, the fame was not positive. Mexicans called them *los diablos Tejanos* (the Texan devils).[1] The U.S. regular army officers reported things they did not like, such as no military uniform and too many weapons.

The Texans had memories of Mexican cruelty. At the Alamo, Ben McCulloch lost his boyhood friend, Davy Crockett. A member of Big Foot Wallace's family was killed at Goliad. Wallace experienced cruel labor in a Mexican prison after the Mier Expedition. The Runaway Scrape and multiple invasions were fresh in their minds. Not everyone handled the situation honorably. The Rangers were reported to be rude bullies, and Mexican towns were afraid of them.

Newspaper cartoon during the Mexican War depicting los diablos Tejanos (Courtesy of the Texas Ranger Hall of Fame and Museum, Waco, TX)

Expert Help

Capt. Jack Hays and his men helped with expert spying and scouting. Big Foot Wallace was frequently in the middle of the action and faced death on his own terms. Once when a Mexican child was trapped in the line of fire, he ran forward, picked it up, and put it over a wall separating the enemies. Then he went back to his side and continued fighting.

Ranger captain Samuel Walker was offered a commission in the U.S. Army and participated in the earliest battles. He was called "the bravest of the brave," and his legacy lives on today. With his help, Samuel Colt improved the Colt Paterson revolver to make the Colt Walker, which the U.S. Army adopted. The first shipment was sent to U.S. troops in the Mexican War. Sadly, it arrived after Walker was killed.[2]

Ranger captain Ben McCulloch, who also served with the U.S. Army, was known for his scouting. The information he gathered was vital in the Battle of Buena Vista. Dressing as a Mexican vaquero, he slipped through enemy lines, spied on the enemy, and then returned with detailed reports. The U.S. won the battle.

Indispensable in Battle

Stories of the Mexican War battles and the wild Texans filled the newspapers back East. Truthful details are difficult to separate from the tall tales. Nevertheless, it's clear that the Rangers were indispensable in battle.

The commander of the U.S. combatants (later president of the United States), Gen. Zachary Taylor, did complain. He said, "The mounted men from Texas have scarcely made one expedition without unwarrantably killing a Mexican."[3] Still, there was no doubt that he used them. They were men who knew the territory. He had skilled American officers, but he needed local information about the enemy, and the Texans fit the need. Many Rangers did the things the regular army did not want to or could not do. In battle, no one fought harder than they did.[4] The U.S. won the war.

The Difference that Reasonable Men Can Make

At the end of the Mexican War, some Rangers near Tehuacan, Mexico wanted a showdown with Santa Anna. News had come that the dictator was leaving Mexico and would travel through a nearby town. Foreseeing danger, Jack Hays, John S. "Rip" Ford, and a few others went to stop a crime.

Rip Ford wrote in his journal that everyone understood the anger. But the leaders talked their comrades out of murder. They reminded the men that the world had come to "condemn Gen. Santa Anna for his cruel butchery of prisoners." They asked that the men not dishonor Texas with reciprocal brutality. These were the right words to use. The men hated Santa Anna, but they loved Texas more.

Everyone rode to the place where the general would pass by, and the Rangers lined the road. As they watched the open carriage go by, no one said a word. When the carriage was gone, Santa Anna passed into history.[5]

Rugged Life Continued

After the Mexican War, the Texas Mounted Volunteers (Texas Rangers) returned to their usual service. Rangers could be used for new purposes. Sometimes they were sent to show official strength or act as interpreters as an Indian peace treaty was drawn up. Ranger Capt. J. B. McGown was one of these men.[6] At treaty meetings, he guarded the U.S. Indian agent. Also, the men were frequently used for fights with the Indians near the Red River (in the north) and in response to border trouble in the Nueces Strip (in the south).

Texas Rangers still had to be ready to do what needed to be done. These men lived a hard, Western-frontier life. Often the Ranger had to go back to using his own supplies. He had to wait for reimbursement while the policies and the money were worked out. That was all well and good until ammunition ran out. When the food was gone, the Rangers hunted. Their goals were fulfilling the mission and survival.

Until around 1858, the men tended to be used less. They were needed but money was scarce. Texas still insisted that the U.S. should pay, and Washington, D.C. still disagreed. The Rangers continued to work on an as-needed basis.

Similar to the early years, support depended on who was politically in charge. From 1847 to 1849, Gov. George T. Wood called on the Rangers only when the U.S. military suggested it. One such instance followed several Indian attacks that occurred between Corpus Christi and the Rio Grande. When thirty-six people were killed, injured, or captured and over a thousand horses were stolen, a U.S. general requested three Ranger companies.

Gov. Peter Bell used the units for emergencies from 1849 to 1853, still insisting that the U.S. pay. Before 1851, there were five companies, each with seventy-nine men. The commanders were Maj. Rip Ford and Captains Big Foot Wallace, J. B. McGown, Henry McCulloch, and R. E. Sutton. They became famous in Texas Ranger history.

Gov. Elisha Pease had six local companies organized. Gov. Hardin Runnels organized the state force, for the edge of the frontier.

Trouble on the Northern Border

In 1858, Indian attacks were coming from north of the Red River. Comanche assaults became bloodier and bloodier in North Texas. Governor Runnels promoted Ranger Rip Ford to senior captain, the supreme commander of the state forces. He was the man to take control.

Rip Ford was originally a doctor. As a Texas Ranger, he fought in many Indian battles and the Mexican War. Ford called his men the Cavalry of the West.[7] He was a thinker and strategist. When people spoke, he paid attention to their words. This Ranger had a calm nature. "Rip" stood for "rest in peace."[8]

As commander, he placed Ranger companies where they would do the most good. He recognized his responsibility to all. At this point in their history, a Ranger captain was the recruiter, supplier, commander, and disciplinarian. In Captain Ford's case, he was also the family consoler. He wanted families of the fallen to know that their loved ones now rested in peace.

Ford decided it was time to stop Comanche chief Iron Jacket's deadly attacks on the citizens of Texas. Ford gathered Ranger units and Indian reserves. He crossed the Red River; Iron Jacket's settlement was north of Wichita Falls. The Rangers and their allies (the Anadarko, Waco, Caddo Confederation, Ioni, Tawakoni, and Tonkawa) attacked. Iron Jacket and more than seventy Comanche warriors were killed, in one of the last battles in this area. Ford succeeded in ending the Comanche attacks.

Southern Border

By 1859, the Rio Grande had troubles again. Cattle rustling became common, and it was sometimes traced to wealthy men. Even after the Treaty of Guadalupe Hidalgo (ending the Mexican War), the Nueces Strip was claimed by more than the U.S.[9] One claimant was a wealthy man named Juan Nepomuceno Cortina. He took over Brownsville in the name of the Republic of the Rio Grande and sought to control the entire Nueces Strip. Cortina had no tolerance for anything that got in his way. He did not acknowledge U.S. laws or Mexican authorities. The battles that resulted were called the Cortina War.[10]

Cortina harmed Texans and some citizens of Mexico. Governor Runnels sent Ford to the Rio Grande Valley with fifty-three of his men. For a time, a relative peace returned to the valley.

Ranger Lawrence Sullivan Ross and Cynthia Parker

Lawrence Sullivan "Sul" Ross was the governor of Texas from 1887 to 1891. He was a "soldier, statesman, knightly gentleman." Sul Ross was a member of the Texas Cavalry, a Civil War general, and a Texas Ranger.

While a Ranger, he helped return Cynthia Parker from her Comanche captivity.

In May of 1836, Indians attacked Fort Parker (near present-day Mexia, Texas). Many people were killed and several kidnapped. One kidnap victim was nine-year-old Cynthia Parker.

Twenty-five years later, Ranger Ross and others came upon a group of Comanche. The Rangers gave chase, killed some, and captured others. Afterward, Ranger Tom Killiheir was yelling at a captured woman. Ross said, "Why, Tom, this is a white woman; Indians do not have blue eyes."[11] The identification was correct. It was Cynthia Parker, all grown up.[12]

Confederate State in the Civil War

Texas seceded from the Union in February of 1861 and became a part of the Confederate States. Many problems had led to this terrible division of families and countrymen. The divisions within Texas were just as numerous and emotional.

The "Father of Texas," Sam Houston, opposed secession and this made him unpopular. The state sent any money and weapons it could to help the South. Many Rangers volunteered to fight for the Confederacy. They were soldiers now and no longer active Texas Rangers.

Gov. Edward Clark created the Frontier Regiment for defense while the Rangers were gone.[13] The regiment was extremely limited, and the Comanche took advantage of the reduced protection to push eastward. They forced the boundary of established Texan settlements back almost one hundred miles.[14] The regiment continued service until the men were drafted into the Confederate ranks (late 1863).

In 1864, Gov. Pendleton Murrah created the Frontier Organization. Protection now lay in the hands of ranging militia and any citizen with a weapon. After the Civil War, the surviving Texans came home. It would take nine years for a Ranger force to be reestablished.[15]

Reconstruction

Historians refer to the Civil War as the U.S.'s most costly conflict. It cost money, lives, and more. Families all over the nation were in pieces. The wounded, exhausted, or broken-spirited soldiers, North and South, made their way home. The highest cost was the pain of citizens killing other citizens, as the indivisible nation was divided.

The South was now in tatters. During the years that the men were at war, the land had not been worked. It lost profit, and the South was bankrupt. Fertile ground *can* come from ashes, but it takes time. For the South, that time was Reconstruction. The Reconstruction Acts set up requirements for the defeated states to meet in order to be readmitted to the Union. Designed to heal, the acts squelched certain states' rights and put Northern representatives in control of Southern states.

In 1870, the state was officially accepted back into the Union. At that time, Republican Edmund Davis became governor. Texas would be under the strict control of the U.S. military—no other organization was allowed to be armed. The U.S. Army now handled all problems in the state.[16] Still, groups of people rose up against crime and tribal attacks or to exact revenge. Others organized solely for protection.

State Police

Governor Davis was not liked. However, he was the one who had the authority to set up Reconstruction requirements in Texas, which included creating the State Police to help maintain Union control in a defeated Confederate Texas. The State Police was made up of both white and black officers. Indian attacks were left to the army to handle.

Davis was considered a carpetbagger governor. He was not from Texas. "Carpetbagger" meant someone who packed his bag and came South to take advantage of the defeated people. Governor Davis stole $34,000 from public funds when he left office.[17] He showed little loyalty to Texas, and the feeling was mutual. He had decided he needed the State Police to enforce the laws. Texans liked this even less.

One man was in both the State Police and the Texas Rangers. Leander H. McNelly became Captain McNelly of the Ranger Special Force. He was a courageous leader who would play a big role in the times of the banditos.

He did not have a man in his company that wouldn't have stepped in between him and death.

Ranger Bill Callicott, one of Capt. Leander H. McNelly's Rangers[18]

Chapter 7

Return to Service

I am conscious of having done all that I could and in the manner best calculated, from a moral as well as legal standpoint, to restore peace and quiet and enforce the law in this community.

Maj. John B. Jones, commander of the Frontier Battalion, 1874

Reorganization

After the Civil War and Reconstruction, the United States began to heal. Texas still had old troubles and continually needed defense. In early 1874, the legislature reauthorized ranging units. Then the new governor, Richard Coke, formed two groups. This was one of the first steps in transitioning Texas Rangers from mounted volunteers to official peacekeepers.

The Frontier Days

The Texas Rangers were changing, but fortunately they had strong leaders to handle the still-wild frontier.

John B. Jones' family arrived in Corsicana, Texas from South Carolina when he was a toddler. He became a terrific horseman who was "at one with the horse."[1] In the Civil War, Jones rose through the ranks from private to major. Then he became the Texas Ranger Frontier Battalion commander.

Controlling so many men required toughness. He was a great leader who was able to listen to others. He knew when to observe and when to speak.[2] He sympathized with them and determined what should happen next. His personality earned the respect of his men.

As the Frontier Battalion executive, Ranger Jones saw the organization as a whole. He put the companies where they were needed, to deal with lawbreakers such as bandits, cattle rustlers, or horse thieves and dangers such as riots, feuds, or general unrest. Major Jones was recognized as "the right man for the right place."[3] He guided the new direction of Texas Rangers law enforcement.

Maj. John B. Jones, commander of the Frontier Battalion (Courtesy of the Texas Ranger Hall of Fame and Museum, Waco, TX)

Major Jones' Two Units

Jones set up two units. One was the Frontier Battalion, for the rough western territory.[4] The other was the Special Force, to protect the south and southwest: the Nueces Strip. The Rangers' objective was to defend territory.

Even with previous decisive battles, the Battalion still had to face an old problem: Indian raids. The Battalion covered the region from the Nueces River up to the Red River in the north, including the Panhandle. This area is larger than some countries. It was not easy covering such a vast region, but the Frontier Battalion was well organized and Major Jones' strategies were very effective.

The Special Force

The Special Force was primarily tasked with fighting banditry. Capt. Leander McNelly was its commander. Mexican banditos were burning ranches to the ground. They were stealing whole herds of cattle and then selling them.[5] Herds were moved deep into Mexico or shipped to foreign buyers (such as Cuba).

Other rustlers were smalltime bandits (American and Mexican). They stole here and there, to gain wealth and territorial rights.

Ignored Orders

Captain McNelly and his Special Force participated in the Las Cuevas War.[6] The captain wanted to cross into Mexico to squelch bandit raids, permanently ending the cattle rustling and related murders. His superiors told him not to go into Mexico, but he proceeded with plans to attack a ranch there that served as the bandito headquarters.

McNelly's Rangers entered Mexico and stormed a ranch. It was the wrong ranch. Several people were killed. He still wanted to attack the headquarters ranch, but the element of surprise was gone. Soon McNelly and his men were being chased by bandits, local people, and Mexican forces.

When the Rangers reached the Rio Grande again, they could not get across. The river was too deep. A ferry was on the U.S. side, under the control of a U.S. Army commander. He was told not to assist McNelly, since the Ranger had ignored orders. This potentially deadly situation was now McNelly's problem.

Capt. Leander H. McNelly, commander of the Ranger Special Force (Courtesy of the Texas Ranger Hall of Fame and Museum, Waco, TX)

McNelly's Rangers were cornered on the Mexican side of the border. When everything seemed to be going wrong, McNelly's nerve pulled the Rangers through. He sent a message to the Mexicans demanding the return of the stolen cattle. If they did not comply, he would attack. It was a bluff, but it worked. Some cattle were returned. The Mexican officials also turned over some of the bandits.

When pressed into a corner, McNelly turned on his foes and did the unthinkable. Sometimes it worked.

Texas Feuds

Captain McNelly and his men were sent to settle the Sutton-Taylor feud (1874). This feud is infamous in Texas history. It reached its peak when Jim and Bill Taylor shot a Sutton in Indianola (near Victoria, Texas). The feud stirred up all of DeWitt County, with citizens choosing sides. McNelly was sent to quiet the unrest and make sure Taylor went to trial. Without Ranger protection, Taylor would have been killed.

McNelly was a determined man. Whether he was squelching feuds or bringing murderers to justice, he focused on his target and let no obstacle get in his path. His strength of mind and courage inspired his men to follow him anywhere. His ways were tough—no bandit wanted to be caught by McNelly's Rangers. According to those who served under his command, he cared for his men but was unforgiving to any lawbreaker.

J. Lee Hall served under Captain McNelly in the 1870s. Hall was named his replacement when the captain became too ill to continue. The Special Force needed an assertive replacement, and Ranger Hall was their man. In 1881, the Special Force became part of the Frontier Battalion.[7]

Frontier Battalion vs. John Wesley Hardin

Those who act outside the law are outlaws. One of the worst was John Wesley Hardin. Some say he was so mean that he shot a man for snoring.

Hardin is touted as the worst killer of the Old West. Whether that is true or not, he killed at least thirty-one men. He racked up these murders by the age of twenty-two. He did not respect the state or the lives of its citizens. This man was dangerous. He became a wanted man, dead or alive.

Hardin eluded lawmen for years. He always seemed to get away. When he killed a deputy sheriff, the Rangers were called. Hardin heard this and left the state.

When a crime is committed in Texas, Rangers can pursue, even into another state. Then they bring the suspect back to face justice. In 1877, Ranger John B. Armstrong followed Hardin east. He found the criminal boarding a train in Pensacola, Florida. Hardin spotted Armstrong and knew he was in trouble. "Texas, by God!" he shouted.

Assisted by local authorities, Ranger Armstrong (later a captain) captured the murderer. During the event, Armstrong faced five outlaws yet subdued Hardin, himself. The Ranger got a bullet hole in his hat but was unharmed. He and his captive returned to Texas.

Hardin was held under Ranger guard until trial. It was rumored there was a plan for a jail break. Armstrong made it known that if anyone tried to escape, there would be consequences. He declared he would kill Hardin and as many jail breakers as he could. Hardin had dangerous enemies, so the Rangers were also his protector.[8]

Sam Bass

Sam Bass was another famous criminal. He was a different kind of villain: an outlaw admired by the common man. People did not exactly think he was good, but they tended to think he was not so bad.

Bass was friendly to those he wanted to befriend. He was considered a Texas Robin Hood. Leaflets told stories about him and songs were written about his escapades. He made a name for himself in Texas, even though he was from Indiana. He stole from banks and railroads, then he spread a little of the money around. This is probably why it took so long to catch him.

Then in 1878, his gang tried to rob one too many banks. A Round Rock bank would be his last target. Texas Rangers had used one of Bass's gang as a spy. Four gang members were shot before the robbery, two went to prison, and one committed suicide. Bass died of his wounds.[9]

Patrols on the Edge of Civilization

The Frontier Battalion started with one company, then two, then more. Finally six companies patrolled the edges of civilized Texas. They had fewer Indian fights but many adventures between 1874 and 1900. There were also some mistakes. Hollywood's Wild West movies reflected this time.

Captains gathered frontier patrols, with each new Ranger bringing a horse and weapon. The recruits were mostly unmarried young men coming from the areas they would protect. They had to be willing to leave home for long periods of time. It was a dangerous job that could take them to the Panhandle or the western plains. They might have to go to the piney woods or the Mexican border.

Trains were just beginning to spread west. They were not always available. So, often the Frontier Battalion had to load wagons with supplies, food, and water, taking a week to cross the state.

Supply and Support

Ranger companies were units on the move. They would set up little camp towns that had their own materials, supply wagons, and specialists. The Rangers cooked their food or had a company cook and chuck wagon. They might have a makeshift hospital.

Basic items were issued to a camp. Bacon, beef, coffee, onions, potatoes, rice, salt, pepper, flour, sugar, soda, candles, and soap were standard supplies. The men occasionally added their own provisions, and when they needed more, they improvised. They fished, hunted, or gathered honey. The Rangers could trade for fresh eggs, bread, or milk at a nearby settlement. Even back in 1875, though, they had to keep receipts.

The Frontier Battalion Rangers used pack mules to carry things from pans

Texas Ranger Frontier Battalion Company E, 1892: 1. Capt. J. S. Mcneel, 2. D. S. Robinson, 3. John Cameron, 4. Charles Johnson, 5. Luke Dowe, 6. P. J. McNeel (not a Ranger), 7. Rigdon Terrell, 8. Forest Townsley, 9. J. S. McNeel, Jr., 10. Everett E. Townsend, 11. Richard Flowers (not a Ranger), 12. Charles Premont, 13. Bud Rader, 14. Louis Pauli, 15. Rut Evans, 16. Bob Townsley (Courtesy of the Texas Ranger Hall of Fame and Museum, Waco, TX)

to ammunition boxes. The animals were able to climb narrow mountain trails. But mules meant extra mouths to feed. They were also noisy, prone to buck, and sometimes scared other animals.

Frontier Battalion Texas Rangers had to take care of their basic transportation, which was the horse until the early 1900s. When possible, they could visit a blacksmith for upkeep and supplies. As the railroad moved west, Rangers could take a train if it went to their destination. Missouri Pacific railroad passes were occasionally provided to them.

Receipts had to be kept, even for ammunition, so that Rangers could be reimbursed up to a certain amount. They had to return any government-provided armaments when their service ended. From one governor to another, reimbursements did not always come. The faithful made do.

Adjutant General

Texas Ranger authority belonged to the state's adjutant general (AG). The process had changed very little. In statehood times, the AG's boss was the governor. He was the one who provided or denied requested supplies. The Texas Rangers were not the military and not the local authority. They were used for special difficulties. AG support fluctuated, but Rangers took the job in good faith and held it through their loyalty.

The quartermaster (QM) was the AG's supply officer. He received his orders from his boss and then fulfilled them. This included both supplies and pay. Everything went down the chain of command.

AGs and QMs were the links between the state authority and the Rangers. It stayed this way until the Department of Public Safety took responsibility of the Rangers in 1935. Rangers handled their needs themselves when necessary. Their purpose went deeper than earning a salary.

The Law and Discoveries

The Rangers continued to scout, trail, fight, and show a force to potential offenders. Railroads expanded and people continued coming to the state. Communication, however, was still by handwritten letter. This meant that a crime might be old news by the time the Rangers got the message. When the telegraph system and then the telephone were invented, information transmission sped up.

Communities and settlements were becoming towns, and towns were turning into cities. Tribal attacks were now uncommon. The Rangers' work tended to involve catching bank robbers, cattle rustlers, and horse thieves. When called, the Rangers were the law, to settle down the lawless.

Capt. G. W. Arrington was the strict leader of his Ranger company. If his men became drunk and unruly, they were jailed like other outlaws. In 1880, Arrington was ordered to search the Texas Panhandle following a report of Indians stealing horses at the Slaughter Ranch. As his unit scoured the territory, they discovered essential waterholes. This important find allowed the Panhandle settlements to expand and led to more ranches.

The last battle between Texas Rangers and tribal peoples occurred in 1881. Then Central and East Texas feuds and other crimes took the forefront.

Fence Cutters

At first there were no fences in Texas. As more and more people settled there, they began to erect fences. To some, these fences, often barbwire strung between posts, were a symbol of tyranny.

Often, those who opposed fences could no longer get their animals to water or pasture. Others just hated the whole idea of fencing off land, and they began to cut the fences in protest. For the most part, the "fence likers" were farmers, and the "fence haters" were ranchers. Texas Rangers were the law between them.

A cut fence meant one more expense for the farmer. When fences were cut, cattle could roam free and ruin the planted crops. It could also result in helpless animals getting tangled up in sharp coils of cut wire. A "fence cutter" is, essentially, someone who vandalizes. That crime was hard to catch in progress and required stealthy detective work. It became such a problem that Rangers were assigned to solve it.

In 1888, Navarro County (south of Dallas) was plagued by fence cutters. Two young Rangers, Ira Aten and Jim King, were sent. They were to go undercover, so that they could identify the criminals. The fence cutters were a tightknit group and it took time to infiltrate them. Even then, the names of the guilty were not certain. So Aten devised a trap within a trap.

Ranger Aten knew that while he seemed to be trusted, there were fence-cutter secrets that no one would share. Communication with Ranger headquarters was by telegraph. He used the close community and his telegraphed messages to catch the guilty. Aten wrote his captain that he had designed a fence-cutting booby trap. He went into details about the dynamite he used, which would explode if anyone tried to cut this particular fence but not if a cow touched it. He said the bombs were scattered but hidden, and he was sure that the guilty party would not escape an explosion.

Whether this is truth or fiction, Aten (later Captain Aten) found a way to stop the violence by using the telegraph and his brain. Fence-cutting incidents declined.[10]

Changes on the Horizon Again

Frontier Battalion Rangers were sort of a cross between mounted police officers and Western mountain men. They had long stretches of nothing to do, leading to boredom and sometimes trouble. They had strengths and faults, and occasionally a man's faults were greater than his strengths. He was removed from the force, but not many were.

The Frontier Battalion lasted for more than a quarter of a century. It stood between citizens and danger. It did its job and its enemies knew it. However, the times and the organization were about to change again.

Arrested John Wesley Hardin, Pensacola, Florida, this pm. He had four men with him. Had some lively shooting. One of their number killed. All the rest captured. Hardin fought desperately. Closed in and took him by main strength.

Ranger Sgt. John B. Armstrong[11]

Chapter 8

A New Century

No man in the wrong can stand up against a fellow that's in the right and keeps on a-comin'.

Texas Ranger Capt. W. J. "Bill" McDonald (Ranger Creed)

The Twentieth Century

The twentieth century started with some old problems. Many new ones would soon show up too. Indian troubles were history—the difficulties were on the border.

Frontier Battalion days were fading away, and the Texas Rangers were in a new age. Border problems made recruiting and maintaining a force difficult. The organization was regrouped into four companies, and their commanders were called the Four Great Captains: McDonald, Rogers, Brooks, and Hughes.

The Four Great Captains

William J. McDonald was from Mississippi, but when he was fourteen, his family moved to Henderson, Texas. He went to college then worked his way from grocer, to deputy sheriff, to deputy U.S. marshal, to Texas Ranger.

In 1891, McDonald was selected as the captain of Company B in Amarillo, Texas. He showed great bravery in the face of violence. He was also known for his one-liners. He probably originated the "one riot, one Ranger," saying, and he is the author of what has become the Ranger Creed.

John H. Rogers was a Texan by birth. His family was poor, and he joined the Rangers to help make ends meet. Twice in his long service, he was badly wounded. He adapted and kept on serving. Rogers became the captain of Company C at Fort Hancock, Texas.

Captain Rogers held strong Presbyterian beliefs. He exerted his authority through quiet example. Villains who assumed he was weak were wrong and came to know their mistake.

Capt. W. J. "Bill" McDonald, one of the Four Great Captains (Courtesy of the Texas Ranger Hall of Fame and Museum, Waco, TX)

John A. Brooks was born in Bourbon County, Kentucky. At twenty-one, he came to Laredo, Texas, where he worked as a coalminer, then a cowboy. Next he became a Ranger. Young Ranger Brooks was badly injured in a battle and lost two fingers. Yet in 1901 he became the captain of Company A in Alice, Texas.

After his service, Brooks was elected to the state legislature. Later on, a

Capt. John H. Rogers and Capt. John A. Brooks, two of the Four Great Captains (Courtesy of the Texas Ranger Hall of Fame and Museum, Waco, TX)

Capt. John R. Hughes, one of the Four Great Captains (Courtesy of the Texas Ranger Hall of Fame and Museum, Waco, TX)

Texas county was named for him. He served as the Brooks County judge until his death.

John R. Hughes was born in Illinois. He worked as a cowboy in Kansas and then the Indian Territory. There he lived among the Choctaw, Osage, and Comanche Nation. Then he purchased a small Texas ranch, working it until he became a Ranger. After dedicated service, Hughes was given command of Company D at El Paso, Texas.

Even before the turn of the century, in 1889, Hughes made dental impressions for identification. Investigation techniques such as these are often thought to be modern, city methods. However, Western criminologists of the nineteenth and early twentieth century were already using evidence to make their cases.

The Four Great Captains started in one century and made a lasting impact on the next. They handled the rough edges of Texas and continually protected its citizens, putting duty before self. In their era, Texas was turning into a new kind of state. Horses and stagecoaches were still necessary, yet trains and eventually automobiles began to take their place. Use of electricity and telegraph would soon lead to telephones. Weapons were improved with interchangeable parts. The biggest change, though, was the population. It grew faster than anyone could imagine. Rangers were needed, and the Four Great Captains were models of the best.[1]

The ranging lawmen had become border fighters and now were becoming law enforcement. This time they faced the overflow of violence from the Mexican Revolution, World War I, and Prohibition. But first, there was the weather.

The 1900 Storm

On September 8, a powerful hurricane slammed into the Gulf Coast of Texas, nearly wiping the island city of Galveston off the map. The third richest city in the U.S. (at that time) was completely covered by water. The 1900 Storm swept away two-thirds of its structures and devastated the inland prairie too. Three-story homes were washed off their foundations and whole families disappeared. Estimates are that 6,000 people were killed, but it was probably more. U.S. soldiers and Texas Rangers were sent to the coast to maintain law and order.[2]

1886-1934

TEXAS

1888
Fence-cutter problems in Navarro County

1900
Sept. 8 The 1900 Storm devastates Galveston, kills at least 6,000

1901
Spindletop oil strike

1917
Gov. James Ferguson impeached

1934
Bonnie and Clyde rampage

UNITED STATES

1901
25th president, William McKinley, assassinated; Theodore Roosevelt becomes president

1903
Wright Brothers flight at Kitty Hawk, NC

1920
Prohibition begins

1929
The Great Depression begins

THE WORLD

1887
Work begins on the Eiffel Tower

1914
World War I begins

1917
Bolshevik Revolution in Russia

1933
Adolf Hitler made chancellor of Germany

Mexico

The Rio Grande forms Texas's border with Mexico for over 650 miles. Soon Mexico would be in turmoil. For the people of the Nueces Strip, the politics and history of the two nations multiplied the difficulties.

Mexico was relatively stable for the first ten years of the twentieth century. Dictator Porfirio Diaz had come to power, by revolution, in 1877, and he held things together for nearly thirty-five years. He expanded the government forces, called *Rurales.* But in 1910, Mexico descended into chaos again.

The Mexican Revolution continued for the next ten years. Between 1911 and 1921, the country had eleven "presidents." They came into office through revolution and sometimes murder.

In those years, again, the Rio Grande was a hotspot. Fear, ignorance, and prejudice simmered on both sides. The border problems reminded people of old injustices, and hatred was sometimes passed down from generation to generation.

The Border

During the Mexican Revolution, the Texas Rio Grande Valley was a place where anyone could be attacked. Incidents occurred in any combination: between Americans, between Americans and Mexicans, and between Mexicans. These border assaults might happen for an actual reason or by mistake. The mistakes were usually committed in the heat of emotion. Whatever the cause, there were many murders, and this dangerous place needed order. When local authorities called for help, the governor assigned Texas Rangers to them as special-duty units.

Bandits and Cattle Rustlers

Bandits caused constant trouble on both sides of the Rio Grande border, attacking settlements, ranches, and haciendas. They struck quickly, often in areas of low population. As the cattle business increased, so did the banditry. By the twentieth century, the bandit problem was unrelenting. The thieves came from different cultures, but they had violence in common. Texas Rangers had dealt with border problems from the beginning. They knew the territory and the job. They were there, on the Texas side of the border, when called upon.

Some bandits specialized in cattle rustling, repeatedly targeting big ranches. Ranchers branded their cattle to help identify them as their property. However, rustlers learned to rebrand over the original mark.

The land in South Texas is perfect for grazing cattle, and huge Texas herds have tempted thieves for over 150 years. The King Ranch has thousands of head of cattle on hundreds of thousands of acres of land. It is hard to watch over it all. Because of the cattle rustlers, this territory has called many times for Texas Rangers to help.

In 1902 three Texas Rangers, under Captain Brooks, were guarding the King Ranch pastures. They came upon a ranch hand who did not seem to be in the right place. He was with another man who was branding a calf. The man branding the calf pulled out "two six-shooters, fired at [the Ranger], but the Ranger's horse shied at the click of the weapon." The Ranger shot back and the man was killed. That man turned out to be Ramon De La Cerda, whose family owned a little ranch next to the King Ranch. He now seemed guilty of theft and attempted murder. The fact that Ramon was a Mexican American and the Ranger was Anglo complicated matters.[3]

Ramon De La Cerda's death led to several other deaths and two inquests. One formal inquest concerned the Ranger, and at least three more killings. The Ranger was cleared. The other inquest, which was unofficial, looked into possible suffering at the hands of the Rangers. This deepened the division between the Anglo and non-Anglo communities.

The newspapers publicized the disputes, and tempers flared on both sides. In two separate incidents, a Ranger either whipped or slapped someone who was maligning or threatening him. This made matters worse and there was more bloodshed.

Texas Ranger W. Emmett Robuck was shot and died. At this point, Captain Brooks took over the investigation. The questioning led to De La Cerda's brother and five other men.

A mob formed, with the intent to lynch the six. Captain Brooks explained that they would have to kill him and every Ranger in Brownsville before he would turn the prisoners over. This was the kind of man he was: ready to die to protect the men accused of murdering one of his own. Captain Brooks proved that Rangers stood for protecting Texans, the state, and the law.

De La Cerda's brother was released on bond, but not for long. He was murdered in Brownsville by the Ranger who shot Ramon. That Ranger took the law into his own hands. Three days later, a potential witness for the Ranger was killed. It was a nightmare.

Gov. Joseph Sayers ordered another investigation. It was proved that some Rangers had slapped or punched members of a threatening crowd. The grand jury also commended Captain Brooks for his service.

Brownsville Affair

In 1906, black U.S. Army soldiers came to the Rio Grande Valley. On the train, they were told they would not be welcome in Texas. They stepped off the train into a segregated section of Brownsville.

Seventeen days later, a bartender was killed and a policeman injured. Many Brownsville citizens blamed the black soldiers stationed at Fort Brown. Nine days later, Capt. Bill McDonald arrived. He walked right into the fort with Ranger W. J. McCauley, and twenty armed soldiers met them. Even though Captain McDonald was told to halt, he continued to approach them. Then he ordered, "Put up them guns!"[4]

In the days that followed, McDonald talked the army into letting him investigate the murder. Then he asked for and received warrants for the arrest of twelve soldiers and one ex-soldier. But McDonald was not allowed to arrest them. Gov. S. W. T Lanham ordered him to let the local authorities handle things. Captain McDonald obeyed.

Prohibition

In 1920, a new national law came along that would keep the Texas Rangers busy for years. The Eighteenth Amendment, otherwise known as Prohibition, outlawed the sale or manufacture of alcoholic beverages. Transporters and sellers of alcohol were now arrested. Law agencies had to tear down bootlegging (homemade manufacturing) operations and confront organized crime, which was making money and causing violence through its lawbreaking. In 1933, the Twenty-First Amendment repealed the Eighteenth Amendment.

World War I

World War I created new assignments for the Rangers, including watching for spies. German moles were known to be in Mexico.

During this time, Mexico's leaders changed from Francisco Carjaval to Venustiano Carranza. President Carranza was pro-Germany, and this made diplomacy difficult with the U.S. German agents were in Mexico, teaching Mexican soldiers. A wireless station transmitted messages from Mexico City to stations controlled by Central Powers (Germany, Austria-Hungary,

Bulgaria, and the Ottoman Empire). With border trouble continuing as before, the U.S. Army and Texas law enforcers were busy.

One Ranger-related incident is recorded from 1918. Capt. Charles F. Stevens was watching the border for spies—a German entomologist, in particular. The Ranger suggested that the bug specialist was developing a way to infect Texas cotton. Captain Stevens warned his superiors about the possible attack on the important crop. It is unclear if he was correct, but the pink bollworm did enter the U.S. from Mexico, through Texas.

In 1919, there were twenty-five racial riots in different parts of the U.S. A fight between white and black mobs took place in Longview, Texas. People were killed and property was destroyed. The governor sent 100 National Guardsmen and eight Rangers to control the violence. After the Texas Ranger investigations, forty-seven people (from both sides) were arrested. The charges were murder and arson.

Political Control

While the world was at war, there was a power struggle in the state too. Political intrigues and wide policy swings from one administration to another made support for the Rangers inconsistent. Each governor used them for his own purposes. For example, Gov. Oscar Colquitt felt that he should select and control the Rangers. He said, "The law places the Ranger Force of the State under direct command of the Governor."[5]

When the governor had integrity, the Texas Rangers reflected it. Less honorable governors often replaced the Rangers who would not follow their wishes. During World War I, Ranger leadership had a quantity of political appointees. For some Rangers, this meant putting loyalty to the governor above duty to the law.

The Fergusons

The early Ferguson years (under Gov. J. E. "Pa" Ferguson) were plagued with problems. There was widespread corruption. The Ranger force was being replaced and expanded by appointees, and most were untrained political supporters. The good, unwavering lawmen were few. But the units that functioned correctly did a great job.

One Texas Ranger who was asked to resign was Capt. John R. Hughes, one of the Four Great Captains. Over half of the Rangers also left. The new force of "Ferguson Rangers" was not of the same standard. Gov. Pa

Ferguson was impeached and removed from office in 1917, and Lt. Gov. W. Hobby was elected governor.

Later, Ferguson's wife, M. A. "Ma" Ferguson, ran and became governor (1925-27, 1933-35). She fired all of the Rangers and appointed over 2,300 "Special Rangers," some of them convicted felons.

Special Rangers

A Special Ranger was a legitimate commission for special service to the state. These commissions had been correctly granted for livestock inspectors, cattlemen, and railroad conductors. When special dangers developed, they were given to shipping officials and former lawmen. It was not a paid position, but the person was authorized to carry a gun.

Ma Ferguson used the special appointments as her husband had done. They were a reward for her supporters, and she gave Special Ranger commissions to whomever she wanted. This included a mortician, a professional wrestler, a dentist, and singer Kate Smith.[6]

Once more, some of the "old stock" stayed with the force.[7] These men preserved the best of the Ranger traditions and followed the legacy. Ranger Capt. Francis "Frank" Hamer was one of them. He served intermittently from 1906 to 1955. From time to time Frank Hamer was a regular Ranger. At other times he had a special commission with the Rangers before Ma Ferguson took office and was a law-enforcement consultant.

Frank Hamer was born a Texan. He grew up in San Saba County and loved the outdoors. "I made up my mind to be as much like an Indian as possible," he said.[8] Trained by two of the Four Great Captains, Frank Hamer improved his detective skills. This prepared him for many pursuits, including tracking down Bonnie and Clyde.

The Texas Ranger force increased during Governor Hobby's term. His adjutant general, J. A. Harley, checked the backgrounds of the new appointees, such as military-service records, temperance reports, and recommendations of good character. The requirements were high again.

Gov. P. Neff was sworn into office in 1921. His most important problems were oil boomtowns and Prohibition crimes. The Rangers helped with both.

Boomtowns

On January 10, 1901, oil burst through the ground from a well at Spindletop, Texas. The Lone Star State entered the boomtown age. Little towns sprouted overnight near Houston and Beaumont, and with the oil money came crime.

The towns started as oilfield camps; they did not even have streets yet. They grew into communities plagued by gambling, prostitution, and greedy officials. This included the sheriff.

These settlements were in total chaos, with trouble growing every year. Boomtowns such as Borger, Kilgore, McCamey, Mexia, Ranger, Burkburnett, Bridgetown, and Wink frequently needed help.[9] Rangers such as Roy W. Aldrich, Marvin "Red" Burton, Tom Hickman, James McCormick, and Capt. Lone Wolf Gonzaullas were called to keep order and enforce state laws.[10]

The Rangers, honed their law-enforcement skills in boomtowns. These men were sent to raid the illegal gambling establishments and clean up the criminal messes. Even when everything was under control, it rarely stayed that way. After the Rangers left, crimes generally started up again.

In the 1920s, Oklahoma wildcatter Ace Borger struck oil in the Panhandle. He set up the town of Borger, and in three months it had a population of 45,000. This boomtown was a special problem for the Rangers.

Borger's founders wanted to protect their investment and the money that the town made. They installed "Two-Gun" Herwig, a gangster from Oklahoma, as the local tough guy. Borger had a sheriff but he was only a puppet, so everything illegal continued, from theft to murder. During Gov. Ma Ferguson's first term, she wrote the Borger sheriff a concerned letter. He told her the town was fine, because he did not want anyone checking up. Then a teenager was shot, and county authorities asked for the Rangers.

Former Ranger captain Gonzaullas was in the area, acting as an undercover U.S. Prohibition officer. He and others converged on Borger. Six Rangers and several federal agents closed down twenty establishments. Borger was left in Texas Ranger hands for a month. After the town elected a mayor and promised change, the lawmen left, but they would be back.

"Situation desperate" was the message that the local judge sent to new Gov. D. Moody. Three months after the Rangers left, Borger was back in trouble. This time the corrupt sheriff, Borger policemen, and sheriff's deputies were killed. The judge asked for as many Rangers as possible.

Capt. Frank Hamer, of Headquarters Company, was sent to Borger. He took four other Rangers, and they were to stay until order was reestablished. In the following weeks, alcohol stills and slot machines were smashed. Prostitutes were given "sundown orders"; they had to be gone by nightfall.

Texas Rangers Frank Hamer and Tom Hickman, beside a still (Courtesy of the Texas Ranger Hall of Fame and Museum, Waco, TX)

Putting stills out of business during Prohibition (Courtesy of the Texas Ranger Hall of Fame and Museum, Waco, TX)

One hundred twenty-four men were arrested. This was a problem, because the Borger jail was not big enough. Rangers attached a large chain to a wooden beam on the floor and shackled the prisoners to the chain until they could be transferred to the county jail. This system was called a "trotline" (from "trout line").[11] It worked.

Boomtowns caused trouble for a long time. The Rangers kept coming back until they were not needed.

The fact that the Rangers are kept on the move has a wonderfully deterrent influence over thieves, who are unable to keep trace of them and constantly fear being surprised and captured by them.

Texas adjutant general[12]

Chapter 9
The Depression Years

An officer must know the mental habits of the outlaw, how he thinks, and how he will act in different situations.
Frank Hamer

Gangsters

In 1929, the Stock Market Crash brought on the financial stress of the Great Depression. Thieves, embezzlers, and forgers abounded. Murderers, smugglers, and large-scale bullies in general came to Texas to set up shop. Rangers became multi-duty law officers.

Prohibition played right into gangsters' plans. Now they could really make money. Their only competition was other gangs. They made, transported, and sold illegal alcohol at nightclubs and restaurants called "speakeasies."[1]

During Prohibition, some raids found over one hundred barrels of whiskey. They uncovered heating equipment (standalone, attached to tractors, and more), mash (corn or grain start), hops, and syrup for making alcohol.[2] They also found narcotics.

Prohibition ended in December 1933. However, the mobsters were now in Texas and they planned to stay. The Texas Rangers were constantly tracking mob activities. After Prohibition ended, gambling was still a problem, and Texas Rangers identified the hotspots. The most famous were Arlington's Top of the Hill, Sherman's Hi-Lite Club, and Galveston's Balinese Room. From 1935 to 1960, Rangers continually raided them and smashed gambling equipment. Laws were being broken, and Rangers enforce the law.

Bank Robbers

After World War I and Prohibition and into the Great Depression, bank robbing became popular. Texas was making money, but many citizens were destitute. Bank robberies became so frequent that the Texas Bankers Association declared a reward for dead robbers. Signs in banks all over the

Capt. Francis "Frank" Hamer (Courtesy of the Texas Ranger Hall of Fame and Museum, Waco, TX)

state read, "Reward: Five Thousand Dollars for Dead Bank Robbers and Not One Cent for Live Ones."

The intent was to stop robberies. Ranger captain Frank Hamer's investigation showed a different result. Innocent people were being killed for the reward. Posses and false heroes would lure drunks or young men to banks, where they were shot. Lawmen were now looking for robbers and murderers.

Based on the proof he found, Captain Hamer requested that the bankers change the reward. When they would not, he went to the press. He provided three cases as evidence, and the bankers association eventually changed their reward.

Bonnie and Clyde

In 1934 Bonnie Parker and Clyde Barrow made headlines. They were dangerous bank robbers and more. Other gangsters in the U.S. were chased by the FBI, but these two were chased by former Texas Rangers Frank Hamer and Manny Gault. When Gov. Ma Ferguson was reelected, they had resigned from the Rangers.

Texas-born Bonnie and Clyde were bank robbers and thieves who resorted to violence. Clyde murdered at least twelve people. When his gang members were captured and sent to prison, Clyde broke them out and killed a mounted prison guard. This crime-committing couple was out of control.

Lee Simmons, superintendent of the Texas penitentiary, requested a special investigator, and he had one man in mind. Frank Hamer now had a special commission from the state highway patrol to hunt down Bonnie and Clyde.[3] He was requested because of his expertise. Hamer gathered information and lawmen to assist him.

Word finally came from Louisiana that a gang member was ready to betray Bonnie and Clyde. In return, he wanted a pardon in Texas. The Barrow Gang traveled back and forth, state to state, without being caught. Two months went by before they were located.

On Easter, Bonnie and Clyde were near Grapevine, Texas visiting family. As they sat in a stolen car, two motorcycle police officers passed them. Then they turned back. A gang member shot at one officer with a whole ammunition clip from a Browning Automatic Rifle (BAR). Clyde shot the other as he reached for his weapon. The officer was shot again. The dead officers were E. B. Wheeler and H. D. Murphy. It was Murphy's first day on the job.

Criminals Clyde Barrow and Bonnie Parker (Courtesy of the Texas Ranger Hall of Fame and Museum, Waco, TX)

Now everyone wanted Bonnie and Clyde. Frank Hamer asked his friend Manny Gault to help. Others were added to the group. The criminals were finally located, and with the help of Barrow Gang member Henry Methvin, four Texas and two Louisiana lawmen were ready for them.

The officers set a trap, waiting beside a road for two days. Their patience paid off. As Bonnie and Clyde's car came down the road, Methvin's father pretended he was having car trouble. When the criminals stopped to talk to him, a signal was given. One of the Louisiana officers started shooting. Then all the others did too, riddling the car with bullets. Bonnie and Clyde were dead.

Hate, Riots, and Bloodshed

Murder is an awful crime, especially when motivated by racial hatred. In 1919, there were twenty-five racial riots in the U.S. In 1930, Texas and its Rangers faced two special cases. On May 3, a black man attacked a white farmer's wife near the town of Sherman. The man was caught and held for trial. In the meantime, unrest grew in the town and eventually the district judge asked for Rangers.

Capt. Frank Hamer, Sgt. J. B. Wheatley, J. E. McCoy, and J. W. Aldrich arrived the next day. They did their best to protect the courthouse and the accused. However, an out-of-control crowd stormed the building during the trial, intent on murder. The scene was mass chaos.

It became so bad that when the court adjourned, firemen had to take witnesses, jurors, and others out through the second-story windows. The accused was put in a vault for safety.

Three more times the mob rushed the courtroom, demanding the suspect. One rioter declared they were coming in no matter what. Captain Hamer replied, "Any time you feel lucky."[4]

The Rangers fought hard to protect the man, but the mob still managed to set the building ablaze, separating him from the Rangers. Firemen were unable to put out the fire—their hoses had been slashed. When the fire died down, the mob attacked the vault, using dynamite to open it. They found the accused, not burned but not alive.

That afternoon, National Guard troops came, and Lone Wolf Gonzaullas joined the other Rangers. It took 430 soldiers, nine Rangers, and many deputies to control the mob. Sherman was put under martial law until May 24. This horrible event was the worst show of racial hate in all of 1930.

The Texas Rangers were called to protect, and they tried their best. They learned from this incident and adapted.

Three months later, a woman was murdered in Shamrock, Texas. A man confessed to the crime and was arrested. This might have been a quickly solved case, but more trouble was brewing. The man who confessed was black; the woman was white. That stirred up local emotions again. Town mobs made threats, so the county sheriff called for Rangers. Lone Wolf Gonzaullas, J. P. Huddleston, W. H. Kirby, and Bob Goss came rapidly. The Rangers told the mob they would protect the prisoner, no matter what. They were not going to let another "Sherman" take place.

The day came for the prisoner to be taken to the courthouse. He was transferred and carefully escorted by the sheriff, in disguise. Then the Rangers raced their car to the courthouse and unloaded machineguns, rifles, shotguns, pistols, and grenades. Their presence and armament were obvious. The disguised sheriff and the determined Rangers foiled the mob. Because of their actions, the accused was able to have his trial. The man was found guilty, but the county sheriff and Texas Rangers had protected his rights and life.

Whatever Texas needed, that was the Rangers' job.

The gamblers and bootleggers hate Rangers worse than the devil does holy water.

Midland, Texas district judge[5]

Chapter 10

The DPS Takes the Reins

More than any other person, Homer Garrison created a Ranger service responsive to the needs of the twentieth century.

Robert M. Utley, historian and author

A Change for Progress

By the 1930s, there were 6 million Texans, and almost half of them lived in or around cities. Previously, the Texas Rangers had to squelch trouble in desolate places. Now they had to do it in cities full of crime, too.

In 1935, the Texas Department of Safety Commission formed the Department of Public Safety (DPS). This combined the Texas Motor Patrol (the Highway Department) and the Department of Motor Vehicles. The Texas Rangers were no longer under the authority of the adjutant general. They had a new boss: the director of the DPS. All this became official through the state legislature on October 10.

Some Texans thought it would mean the end of the Texas Rangers. In truth, it helped preserve the organization and its traditions. Within the first few years, the DPS established a crime lab. It gave the Rangers a strong support system, and this was only the beginning.

The DPS provided the Rangers with a permanent headquarters in Austin. They were officially recognized in the state law books as a crime-fighting force. Many innovations came to the Texas Rangers, and new traditions were made.

When the DPS took over, the organization now had a chain of command separate from political administrations. There were still political pressures, but a new administration no longer meant a total Ranger restructuring. This allowed them to concentrate on protecting Texas.

Garrison Rangers

Homer Garrison was the third director of the DPS. He restored, protected, and guided the Texas Rangers to a new age, shaping them into

1935-1999

TEXAS

1935
DPS created

1940
Lone Ranger movie serials popular

1961
Hurricane Carla hits Gulf Coast

1963
NASA's Manned Spacecraft Center opens in Houston

1999
FBI 10 Most Wanted List serial killer Rafael Resendez-Ramirez is captured in El Paso

UNITED STATES

1941
December 7 Pearl Harbor is attacked; U.S. enters World War II

1958
First microchip developed

1963
President Kennedy is assassinated

1969
Astronauts Neil Armstrong and Buzz Aldrin step onto the moon

1972
Watergate scandal

THE WORLD

1939
World War II begins

1948
Country of Israel founded

1950
Korean War begins

1961
Russian cosmonaut Yuri Gagarin is first human to orbit the earth

1989
Berlin Wall comes down

Twentieth-century law-enforcement officers. The DPS was now helping to supply whatever they needed, such as weapons, cars, radios, and other communication devices. They had access to surveillance aircraft and the DPS armored vehicle.

His policies were designed to benefit the whole DPS. He developed training programs that included the Rangers; they learned criminology, crime-lab science, and new weaponry. Colonel Garrison also encouraged independence rather than following standard police practice, which was already a Texas Ranger legacy. These lawmen were perfect for him, and the feeling was mutual. "Mr. Law," as one of his Rangers called him, also made sure that only the best of the best were selected.[1] Standards were set, and the badge was never given lightly. Preparedness and adaptation were like the boots the Rangers wore or the hats on their heads: part of their gear.

Over the years, Garrison upgraded the crime lab. He continually asked the legislature to increase Ranger financing and manpower. He motivated them and fostered camaraderie. Texas Ranger customs and pride were alive and well in the DPS. At this point, a Texas Ranger could make his job a career, without political uncertainty.

These men were now a part of an expert, modern law-enforcement agency.[2] The Rangers brought experience to their work, which was of the highest caliber. DPS resources were able to back that experience.

Science in the Legacy

Ranger captains Samuel Walker, John Hughes, and Lone Wolf Gonzaullas were from different generations. But they shared keen intellects and stubborn determination. They used these qualities, and science, to outthink their foes.

Captain Gonzaullas was just one of the organization's early- to mid-twentieth-century leaders. During the 1930s, he had an oil-boom problem in Mexia. He told that community, "You got one riot, you get one Ranger." He used his version of the old quote to put the people's worries to rest. The Rangers were on the scene now and they could handle the trouble.

Born in Spain, Manuel T. Gonzaullas was perfect for his future job. When Gonzaullas was a young man, Capt. John Hughes was his hero.[3]

A DPS laboratory was created to facilitate the Bureau of Intelligence. Captain Gonzaullas was its chief and a criminal-science expert, conducting lab work, ballistics studies, and fingerprinting. The lab also handled moulage casting, microscopic study of evidence (fabric, hair, blood, and others), and document examination.

Captain Gonzaullas was a handwriting analysis authority. This procedure was vital in investigating kidnapping, extortion, robbery, murder, and terrorism cases.

What he did not know, he found out or developed, then trained others. Gonzaullas created a lab and a staff that rivaled the FBI, who sometimes came to him for help. The Rangers gained access to the DPS forensic laboratories and files, giving them a new edge in their investigative skills.

The Phantom Killer

In 1946, a murderer terrorized the Texarkana area. Four couples were attacked between February and May; five people were killed and three injured. The assailant wore a mask, so survivors could not identify him. Newspapers dubbed him the Phantom Killer.

Rangers worked the case under Lone Wolf Gonzaullas. Unfortunately, curiosity seekers destroyed evidence before it was collected. Captain Gonzaullas's team continued to gather and examine what they could. They took molds of tire tracks and used other investigative techniques.

The forensic knowledge of the DPS was essential. The Rangers worked the evidence, set up protective patrols, and used officers as decoys. The killer was never caught, but with all the Texas Ranger attention, the murders stopped.[4]

Updated Weapons and Transportation

There were twentieth-century changes in the Rangers' weapons too. They were issued the Colt .45 pistol along with the lever-action Winchester .30-caliber rifle. By the year 2000, the Rangers also carried automatic shotguns as standard weapons. The criminals' weapons improved as the decades went on, so law enforcement had to keep up.

When the DPS took over the Rangers, cars had been around for about twenty-five years. At first, each Ranger had to provide his own horse, saddle, and car. One-third of the men received a monthly car allowance of eighty dollars.

The horse was still a regular component of law enforcement in the western part of the state. So when cars came along for those Rangers, so did horse trailers. Today, the Texas Ranger has access to almost any kind of transportation available. While horses are still used, as Lt. George Turner of Company F says, "It's more horsepower instead of horses."[5]

DPS took care of the Texas Rangers' logistics, even for their horses (Courtesy of the Texas Ranger Hall of Fame and Museum, Waco, TX)

Paperwork and a Home

Of course, an upside usually has a downside. Now the Rangers had to do the paperwork. They needed to keep track of their travels (car, horse, airplane, helicopter, or whatever), note expenses, write weekly reports, and record time on and off the clock. This was not a Ranger tradition, but it became one.

This paperwork was needed as possible evidence in their cases. If a prosecutor called for this information to help secure a conviction, a Texas Ranger had to be ready to provide it.

At headquarters, many Texas Rangers found an esprit de corps under Colonel Garrison's direction. They repaid him by working harder and longer. Lewis Rigler, thirty-three years a Ranger, described how the Rangers thought of Garrison. "I have never spoke to one Ranger who served under Homer Garrison who didn't idolize the man—none. And he loved the Rangers . . . the Rangers considered Garrison a Ranger."[6]

Bob Crowder, Johnny Klevenhagen, and James E. Riddles are great examples of Garrison Rangers. They patiently worked during the changing times and gave others the courage to do the same.[7]

Capt. Bob Crowder

Robert Austin Crowder was originally from Minden, Texas. He served in the Marine Corps and later worked in the DPS Bureau of Intelligence. By 1939, he was Ranger Crowder. In 1947, he became a captain.

Ranger Lewis Rigler said his captain was "the type of man others just naturally want to follow . . . but he was never conceited or pompous with it." This was Ranger leadership. It carried the organization through in frightening situations.

One of the scariest problems anyone can face is trying to control a violent person who is mentally ill. If the human brain is not working normally, an aggressive person is unpredictable. Such was the case when a riot erupted in 1955 at the Rusk State Hospital, part of which was a facility for the criminally insane. Eighty-one inmates gained control and took hostages. The peace officer that the DPS sent was Captain Crowder.

Crowder had to solve the problem, save the hostages, and try not to get killed. The patients demanded he come to them, unarmed. "I'm not comin' in unarmed because you've already got three people over there as hostages and I don't want to be the fourth one—and I'm not going to be," he said. "I just want to tell you this. If something goes amiss, I know who's going to fall first."

He said exactly what he felt and what he was going to do. He also gave them consequences to consider. If they understood his clear talking, they might make the right choice. Crowder's words were not just unusual and daring. They were honest and hopeful. They also recognized the prisoners, mentally hindered or not, as human beings. He gave them just as much chance to make a good decision as any other criminal he opposed.

Then Captain Crowder walked to the hospital. He stood alone at the door and talked to the leader of the riot, who was armed with an icepick and a pair of scissors. The Ranger warned the man what would happen if they did not give up, and he promised them a hearing with the hospital director. The inmates came out, piled up their weapons, and let the hostages go. The riot was over.

When DPS director Garrison asked what he said to the inmates, Captain Crowder replied, "Aw, boss, I just told them to cut out that stuff."[8] The fact is that the Texas Rangers are often quiet heroes.

World War II

The 1941 Japanese attack on Pearl Harbor propelled the United States into World War II. The U.S. and other Allied countries were fighting the Axis nations of Japan, Germany, and Italy. For the Ranger, protection efforts again focused on spies and other adversaries.

As before, certain criminals found opportunities for wrongdoing during wartime. When most of the men were gone from home, lawbreakers saw easy pickings among the rest of the population. Crime increased, but Rangers were also called occasionally to track deserters or escaped prisoners of war.

More Mobsters

Texas went through changes in the mid-twentieth century, but one thing that did not change was the presence of mobsters. They were not going to leave on their own. Organized crime syndicates tried to control unions and gambling. Gambling was illegal in Texas, but in the shadows, it was going strong. So Rangers battled the mob.

Gambling was a problem in every part of the state. One of the biggest gambling cities was Galveston, which was like a Las Vegas of the Gulf Coast. The Maceo family controlled little casinos there in restaurants and shopping emporiums. The largest were in nightclubs, frequented by Hollywood performers. At the Balinese Room, which was built on stilt-like pilings on Galveston Bay, tourists came to see the shows, bet, and enjoy the beach. These types of venues made a lot of money and Galveston prospered, even in the Great Depression. Unfortunately, that wealth came from crime. It was time for the Rangers to restore order.

The Gold Dust Twins

In 1957, John J. Klevenhagen became the captain of Texas Ranger Company A, in Houston. He took his duty seriously. He knew every weapon and flew the DPS plane.

Buster Kern was the Harris County sheriff. The two crimefighters were called the Gold Dust Twins,[9] and these leaders and their men worked diligently to close down gambling houses. Almost every time, though, the case fell through. In a week or so, the business would reopen.

Rangers raided the Balinese Room continually, but it presented a special challenge. The club had a long pier leading to the entrance, which gave the proprietors time to hide evidence of illegal activity if any officers approached. The pier was known as "Ranger Run," because the Rangers had to hurry along it to catch gambling at the club. However, when Las Vegas became popular with gamblers, they lost interest in Galveston, and the Balinese Room eventually closed.

Other gambling places in the Houston-Galveston area stayed open. The

Rangers knew where they were, but the wagering activities were hidden. Captain Klevenhagen assigned two of his men every night to a special task. They showed up as customers but in complete Western law-officer gear. They wore their pistols in holsters and their star badges on their shirts. Worried customers left, and after a while, the gambling houses went out of business.

Labor Disputes

After World War II, industrialization spurred a tremendous growth of cities and populations. This caused unions to come to Texas, in full force. Clothing factories, oil companies, and farms became unionized. Steel mills were also big business and now had unions. Unfortunately, there were also strikes. That is when the Rangers were called.

Working a strike was the last assignment that a Ranger wanted. If they were called, that meant the strike could become violent. The Rangers' duty was to uphold the law, protect the citizens, and stop the violence. If the Rangers halted the violence, the strikers were upset. If the protest was not violent, the Rangers kept an eye on things, and then the companies tended to be upset that more was not done. It was a no-win assignment. People could also get killed, including the Ranger.

Capt. Lone Wolf Gonzaullas proclaimed, "The rights of the strikers to peaceful picketing and all other legal means will be upheld just as firmly as the legal rights of the company."[10] Two strikes had a particularly deep impact on Texas and its Rangers.

The first was the Lone Star Steel Company strike near Daingerfield, in 1968. It lasted seven months, and violent attacks occurred throughout that time. Strikers used every weapon imaginable, including fire, rocks, chains, bricks, bottles, nails, wire cutters, knives, guns, fists, automobiles, homemade bombs, and dynamite. Capt. Bob Crowder said later, "We were there to protect both sides, the people coming, the people going, and we weren't going to take sides."[11] Yet he and Ranger Bob Mitchell were almost killed. A pickup truck followed them from the plant one morning and they were shot at, but both Rangers escaped injury. The strike ended in May of 1969.

One strike at several farms in Starr County and La Casita Farms was a long, nasty event. Rangers were called to help. The ordeal started in June of 1966 and continued for almost a year. The judicial cases that related to it were not settled until 1974.

The Texas Rio Grande Valley was rich with farmland. The area was also going through changes. By the summer of 1966, farm union leaders in California were speaking up for the National Farm Workers Organizing Committee (NFWOC), and they were working to unionize the tip of Texas. Soon, eight corporate produce growers in Texas had a strike on their hands, and La Marcha began.

La Marcha was a march to Austin in support of the strike. It began in Rio Grande City, Texas, and the plan was to arrive in the capital by Labor Day. The marchers' slogan was "¡*Viva la huelga!*" meaning "long live the strike." They intended to present their demands to the governor, but sympathetic politicians met with them instead.

When Rangers were finally requested,[12] Colonel Garrison sent Capt. Alfred Y. Allee, Sr., of Company D. His job was to assist the peacekeeping in the Lower Valley. Violence was stirring, and operation of the Missouri Pacific Railroad was threatened. This railroad is vital to transportation and commerce for the whole state and beyond. Two battle lines were forming, with lawyers and politicians on both sides.

Warrants were signed for the arrest of ten picketing union leaders. The Texas Rangers had to do the arresting, but then until May, they stayed in the background. Local authorities were handling the situation.

Then in May of 1967, Captain Allee, his Rangers, and local deputies arrested a number of strikers for blocking a train that was carrying produce. The incident led to investigations, more warrants, chasing suspects, and knocking down doors to locate them. Some citizens complained of police brutality. After a DPS investigation, Col. Homer Garrison said that those claims were "totally false and unfounded."[13] In the end, the NFWOC filed a class-action suit. It pitted seven individuals against four Rangers and six Valley law officers and officials. One of the plaintiffs was Francisco Medrano, and the suit was called *Medrano v. Allee*. This case went all the way to the U.S. Supreme Court. In the meantime, Captain Allee retired in 1970, and Capt. John M. Wood took command of Company D.

Supreme Court Ruling

Medrano v. Allee first went before the U.S. district court. The judges ruled that five of the six complaints were valid. They said that the law officers had "violated the First and Fourteenth amendments."[14]

The state of Texas disagreed and appealed to the Supreme Court on behalf of the defendants. On May 20, 1974, Justice William O. Douglas delivered the majority opinion. The judges found persistent signs of intimidation. They said the defendants "exercised their authority under valid laws in an unconstitutional manner." While the ruling was in majority, four of the justices disagreed with portions of the complaint. Nevertheless, the majority decision of five judges over four held.

Some thought this would be the end of the Ranger organization. There were those who desired this. But the Rangers survived.

I did not think then, or now, that a Ranger has any business working a strike. No matter what we do, we lose.

Ranger Glenn Elliott[15]

Chapter 11

The Last Third of the Twentieth Century

I carry a gun, 'cause a cop is too heavy.
Anonymous Texas Ranger

Politics

The law is to be protected. That is the Ranger's job. Rangers are rarely called to a political protest, but if an angry mob threatens to hurt people, Rangers go where they are needed.

In Zavala County, close to the Mexican border, the La Raza Unida party wanted every vote to be counted in the 1972 election. The established county authorities, not of that party, were nervous about the election. If the votes were as many as the protest indicated, the seated officials might be out of a job. On Election Day, when the county elections judge saw trouble.[1] He sent for help, Ranger H. Joaquin Jackson arrived.

Both sides of the election were agitated. Jackson came to protect the people and the laws of the state, and he did exactly that. He acted as a mediator, and his negotiation allowed two poll watchers from the Mexican-American side of the conflict. They would observe as the elections judge counted the results.

The La Raza Unida candidates won by a landslide. One Texas Ranger had averted a riot. He protected the rights of every voter.

Kidnappings

Abductions are terrifying, for the victim and family. A kidnapping takes away a person's freedom and can have deadly results. This has been a popular crime in America since the 1960s, but Rangers and other support agencies are there to help.

In 1971, Huron Ted Walters pulled a gun on a Euless policeman. When he went on the run, he took Hoyt Houston, his wife, and five-year-old daughter hostage as his safety net. But he was not expecting the Texas Rangers.

The kidnapper forced Mr. Houston to drive him where he wanted to go. Police put up roadblocks, cornering the car near Southlake (between Dallas and Fort Worth). While lawmen distracted Walters, Ranger Tom Arnold of Company B took aim through his rifle scope. At the right moment, he pulled the trigger and then ran to the vehicle. The kidnapper was dead, and the Ranger was able to save the family. Walters had taken the Houston family's freedom and placed them in danger, and he paid the price for his violent mistake. Ranger Arnold gave the Houstons their freedom back.

Serial Killers

The Rangers have met a few serial killers. Henry Lee Lucas was one of the creepiest criminals of the twentieth century. When he was charged with two murders and taken to the Montague County jail (near the Oklahoma border), he bragged that he had killed at least one hundred.

Lucas had been in trouble with the law since the 1960s. Now in 1983, he had the spotlight. He admitted to killing his mother and then 150 others.[2] The press flocked to him to learn more. Police forces around the country saw the potential to solve cold cases.

After spending time with Lucas, Ranger Phil Ryan said, "I've been to two county fairs and a hog-calling, and I've never seen anything like this." Lucas confessed to murder after bloody murder. For three months, Ryan had to listen to descriptions of this madman's crimes. "In one night he goes through forty murders," the Ranger said. "It can't help but affect you if you value human life."[3]

Ranger Ryan met with more than eighty officers from twenty states to compare notes on cases. Early on, he and others recognized Lucas as not just a killer. He was a big liar too. Still, the press kept reporting and investigators kept listening.

That fall, twenty-eight confessions were confirmed, resulting in nineteen arrest warrants. A total of ninety-seven murders had connections to other cases. All this time, Ryan was a one-man task force. After he spent a year hearing confessions and handling the details, an official task force was established, with Ranger Sgt. Bob Prince of Company F in charge.

In March of 1984, Lucas was convicted of murdering an unidentified woman known as "Orange Socks." The jury gave him the death penalty. He had confessed to scores of murders, but now he was telling reporters that he only killed his mother. The media kept Lucas in the headlines, this time raising the possibility of his innocence. Some periodicals even asked if the Rangers had coached his confessions.

Even though Lucas had been convicted, an investigation was made in order to be sure. It found no wrongdoing by the Rangers. In February of 1985, the new senior captain, H. R. "Lefty" Block, said, "These days, we portray a professional image. We don't play games and tricks anymore. We're there to get the job done."[4]

Henry Lee Lucas died of natural causes at the Huntsville, Texas prison in 2001. However, other serial killers would strike again.

Two Rangers, One Kidnapper, and a Little Girl

Another case happened in 1987. A woman was kidnapped near Marble Falls, Texas, tortured, and brutally murdered. She was the maid for the Whitehead family. She was missing for about a week, then on January 22, two-year-old Kara-Leigh Whitehead was kidnapped. Fortunately, many law enforcers began looking for her right away. Two Texas Rangers would save her.

Mr. Whitehead received a ransom demand. He ignored the kidnapper's warning and contacted the authorities. The FBI kidnapping experts and the Rangers had a plan to save Kara-Leigh.

The kidnapper told Mr. Whitehead to get the money and drive his car to the ransom drop. The Whiteheads' car was not big enough for the rescue plan, so a larger car was used, with the backseat removed. Two Rangers would hide in that space.

Rangers John Earl Aycock and Stan Guffey squeezed into the backseat area. It was a dark night, so a dark cloth camouflaged them. Mr. Whitehead drove to the drop-off house. Before he got out, he begged the Rangers to bring his daughter back safely.

The kidnapper put the little girl in the front seat and got in the car. He grabbed the ransom briefcase Mr. Whitehead left on the seat and tossed it in the back. It landed on Aycock, but he said nothing. Then the kidnapper pounded on the case and the cloth slipped a little. Ranger Aycock's face was slightly exposed, and he saw the criminal's gun pointed right at him.

When the kidnapper saw the trap, he jumped from the car. Ranger Guffey identified himself, and the kidnapper fired. Guffey was wearing a bulletproof vest but was struck in the head. He was still able to fire his gun. Ranger Aycock grabbed Kara-Leigh, pulled her out of the way, and fired at the kidnapper. Then he told her, "I'm a police officer, honey . . . a Ranger."[5] The kidnapper's days of violence were over—permanently.

Aycock, and others, tried to help Guffey. Stan Guffey was also John Aycock's friend. Ranger Guffey was barely alive; FBI agents and Rangers took him to the nearest hospital.

Both Rangers had been ready to die to protect the little girl. Sadly, one

Texas Ranger Stan Guffey, posthumous recipient of the Texas DPS Commissioners' Medal of Valor (Courtesy of the Texas Ranger Hall of Fame and Museum, Waco, TX)

did. Texas Ranger Guffey died in the line of duty. Kara-Leigh Whitehead was returned to her parents.

The Branch Davidian Tragedy

In 1993, over a hundred people were living about ten miles northeast of Waco, Texas, in a place just outside Elk, Texas that they called Mount Carmel. It was not Waco but not officially a town. Their little complex was located off the Double E Ranch Road. The people who lived there called themselves the Branch Davidians. By summer, the area would be a murder crime scene.

The Texas Rangers knew that these people followed a fanatical leader named David Koresh. The Federal Bureau of Alcohol, Tobacco, Firearms and Explosives (ATF) thought they knew who the Davidians were too. They had been investigating the group for months. The leader and his associates were suspected of drug involvement, child abuse, and polygamy. The ATF was also sure they were storing huge amounts of weapons.

Finally, the ATF decided to raid the Mount Carmel compound. Ranger Capt. Bob Prince of Company F offered assistance. However, he was told it would be a federal arrest, so the Rangers did not participate.[6]

The next day, injured and dying ATF agents were carried out of Mount Carmel. The Branch Davidians had fought off the federal assault. Four agents were dead and twenty were injured.[7] There were deaths and injuries inside the compound too.[8] Everyone knew that there were women and children in the compound, so this was a serious concern.

It was now a standoff. Koresh's people were literally fighting the government. This dangerous incident was not over, so the federal prosecutor asked the Texas Rangers to investigate. They would explore the raid and the capital murder of four ATF agents. Capital murder means that the perpetrator is eligible for the death penalty.

These peacekeepers were known for their professionalism and thoroughness. They were top criminal investigators, and according to Ranger George Turner, the "prosecutor only wanted the Texas Rangers on the case–no one else." The prosecutor knew they would be objective, trustworthy, and detailed. This is the only time a state organization has investigated a federal agency. The Rangers were up for the job.

For the next fifty-one days, the Davidians and the FBI were locked in a standoff. During that time, the FBI tried to convince Koresh's people to come out. They cut off the electricity and drove military tanks around the compound. The tanks knocked down and crushed objects all over the grounds.

As this was going on, the Texas Rangers were interviewing witnesses. They were collecting evidence and putting all of the pieces together. However, the tanks destroyed much of the outside evidence.

Concern grew for the Davidian children. Fearing more deaths, the FBI pushed to end the standoff. They would use teargas and tanks with battering rams to make the Mount Carmel inhabitants leave.

On April 19, the FBI made an assault. Tanks smashed holes in walls, and teargas was forced through them. Davidians shot at the tanks. Around noon, a fire broke out. Seventy-six people died, including women and children.

All investigation was turned over to the Rangers. Now their job had doubled. The seventy-seven-acre Mount Carmel compound had become a huge crime scene, battlefield, and site of a fire. Evidence was everywhere.

The Rangers found 300 weapons; 48 had been altered to be deadlier. They stored 24,000 pounds of Mount Carmel wreckage. It was all evidence and all sent to Austin for a trial. This time, the ever-ready Rangers were there to protect the proof and be crime-investigation experts. Capt. David Byrnes declared that this task was likely the most important one the Rangers had had in half a century. They were not a part of the raid but they played a major role as expert witnesses. They were impartial observers and collectors and guardians of evidence.

Eight Davidians were convicted of conspiracy. Wrongful-death suits were filed against the government. Seven years later, it was ruled that David Koresh was the person at fault.

Republic of Texas (ROT)

In 1995, a group of people living near Fort Davis, Texas declared they were separate from the rest of the United States. They called themselves the Republic of Texas (ROT). They said that the Lone Star State had been illegally annexed into the U.S. back in 1845. So they decided to make their own country.

They did not respect anyone else's laws, law officers, or tax officials. These supposed "true Texans" lived in Texas but had previously come from other states. They made their declaration to get attention.

In 1997, representatives of the U.S. and state governments ordered a warrant for the arrest of Richard McLaren, the "ambassador" of the ROT. Then he and his comrades made the same mistake that the Branch Davidians did. They threatened harm to the state and federal officials. They announced on their Web site that they would meet the "invasion" with violence.

When a ROT person was arrested (not McLaren), the group retaliated by attacking a home near their compound. Three people held Mr. and Mrs. Joe Rowe at gunpoint. Mr. Rowe was shot in the shoulder and suffered some cuts.

Ranger Capt. Barry Caver was contacted, and he put all of his Company E on alert. They were to meet him in Fort Davis. The local sheriff gave Caver the lead on the case.

When the captain made contact with the group, McLaren denied the attack. Yet the ROT Web site called the Rowes prisoners of war. McLaren also made threatening remarks against the Texas governor and others. Against his better judgment, Captain Caver negotiated the release of the Rowes, so that Mr. Rowe could get medical help.

After a few days, thirty-five Rangers, the local sheriff, and highway patrolmen were at the location. FBI agents, Border Patrol, U.S. marshals, Texas Forest Service personnel, Texas Parks and Wildlife game wardens, and the DPS SWAT team also gathered in the West Texas area. These officers had both equipment and support, including two Fort Bliss Blackhawk helicopters and two armored personnel carriers (APCs), nicknamed Bubba 1 and Bubba 2. Captain Caver also had onsite support from Ranger Chief Bruce Casteel and DPS Director Dudley Thomas. They let Caver retain his lead position.

Captain Caver assigned Jesse Malone as negotiator. Ranger Malone is described as a "man who could talk sensibly with anyone." The ROT talked in confusing language. They did not recognize the real Texas.

Caver had the ROT Web site taken down. McLaren then got on his ham radio, saying, "Mayday! . . . Hostiles are invading the Republic of Texas embassy!" He added that the invaders would be "dead meat."[9]

Finally, after almost a week, the standoff ended. Captain Caver and his support solved the problem.

Manhunt for a Killer

In 1999, lawmen all over the country were looking for serial killer Rafael Resendez-Ramirez. At least one of the murders had been committed in the Houston area. When West University Place (a Houston incorporated community) police asked the Texas Rangers for help, Ranger Sgt. Drew Carter of Company A got the job.

In March, Carter was contacted by Immigration and Naturalization Service (INS) agents and others who were tracking Resendez-Ramirez. This suspect was a forty-year-old illegal alien from Mexico. Sergeant Carter made sure that the man would be stopped if he was being deported or even spotted near the border.

By this time, Resendez-Ramirez had already murdered three people. In the next four months, there was a great deal of interagency cooperation in locating him. Resendez-Ramirez was added to the FBI's Ten Most Wanted list. He was finally caught by the Border Patrol. During those months, though, he committed six more murders. He surrendered in El Paso.[10]

The Rangers did their part and proved that they stay professional when working with other agencies. Former Ranger Sgt. Jeff Cook explained it this way: "We meet up, decide which agency can punish the criminal the best, and they take the lead. There are no arguments like you see [on television]. We are all in this together."[11]

Texas Rangers were now crime fighters, dogged detectives, practiced lawmen, civil rights-aware enforcers, and determined crime-investigating Texans. These qualities were added to the organization's steady traditions.

Silver stars and Sixguns.

Description of the Texas Rangers by Col. Homer Garrison, Jr.[12]

Chapter 12
Texas Ranger Teamwork

A Ranger is an officer able to handle any given situation without definite instructions from his commanding officer or higher authority. This ability must be proven before a man becomes a Ranger.

Ranger Capt. Bob Crowder

A Diverse Group All Along

Texas Rangers may be from different towns or backgrounds, weapons experts or forensics specialists, and male or female. Their outward differences do not matter. What is important is what they have in common. They are a team of multi-skilled law officers. They are dedicated Texans of the highest standard. They are Texas Rangers.

Rangers are unified in their goals, sense of duty, and standards of integrity. Each one is chosen for the same values and able to do any tasks that arise. Every Ranger is at the ready. The thing about the Texas Rangers is that a Ranger is a Ranger. The individual is a part of the whole, and the group is, by design, one Ranger. Their job is providing protection for all Texans. They serve one state, one star.

Other Ages, Other Fights, All Rangers

Even with the bloody fights with Mexico, there were Mexican Rangers before the Battle of the Alamo. There have been many after. They fought for the same republic, as the others, and they have protected the same freedoms. Joseph Lopez, Delores Cortinez, Francisco Acosta, and his commander, Capt. Lewis Sánchez (and most of his unit), are names from the days of Texan independence. The republic and state Ranger rolls list over 150 with Mexican roots.[1] At times, the numbers were in the single digits, but they served.[2]

Settlers battled fiercely with American Indians over territory in early times. Yet American Indians assisted Rangers from the beginning. Many tribesmen served in units to provide defense and protection. They were indispensable for their knowledge and bravery. Alloverbiggness, Buzzard, Flacco, and his commander Castro are examples of names from the unit lists of Ranger scouts. Lipan Chief Flacco worked closely with Jack Hays.[3]

French, Spanish, Scotch, German, Irish, and English names also fill the rosters.

Lady Rangers

The first females to be called rangers were Special Rangers. Their official warrant recognized their authority in special duties. In the 1930s and 1940s, a few women were given this title for their work as government assistants. They dealt with sensitive information. These women were trusted with secrets regarding the security of the governor.

In 1993, females were added to the Texas Rangers regular ranks. Others have been appointed since.

All Rangers are chosen on the same basis. There are no shortcuts to high standards. They are expected and required to do the same duty. They serve with the same fortitude and share the same traditions and responsibilities. The job is bigger than the individual Ranger. They are there to serve.

Rangers Without Limits

No human body is perfect. Everyone has something they can do well and

Arch Miller served better than many two-armed Rangers. From left to right: Pete Crawford, state game warden; Ray Miller (Arch's brother); John Pool; Arch Miller; and Steve Bernett, justice of the peace. (Courtesy of the Texas Ranger Hall of Fame and Museum, Waco, TX)

Rangers H. A. Carnes and Pat Craighead, who stayed in service even after he lost his leg in a 1910 ambush in the Brownsville area (Courtesy of the Texas Ranger Hall of Fame and Museum, Waco, TX)

something they cannot. Sometimes the "cannot" is due to a physical problem. Some people do not let this stop them. Rangers with physical disabilities have served, while others were injured in the line of duty but kept working.

Maj. Robert Williamson became a ranging mounted volunteer in the early days of Texas independence. Polio required him to use a peg leg. Yet he could ride, dance a jig, and fight like the rest of the Rangers. He was as tough as nails and an inspiration.

Erastus Smith came to Texas from New York when he was in his thirties. Unfortunately, an illness had cost him his hearing. From then on, he was known as Deaf Smith. Ranger Smith's scouting talents set the standard for others, especially during the Runaway Scrape.[4]

In 1918, La Fetra Trimble was made a Ranger even though he had a bad eye. The skills he had impressed his commander more than the sight he lacked.

Arch Miller was the only one-armed Ranger. He served in Company G just as well or better than others.[5]

Pat Craighead started his service with two legs but lost a leg in an ambush. Ranger Craighead served for six more years.[6]

All of these men were Rangers, and all Texas Rangers go above and beyond the call of duty.

Families with Their Own Legacy

Texas Rangers are surrounded by tradition. Sometimes that means following in a father's, uncle's, or brother's footsteps.

Captains Benjamin and Henry McCulloch were Ranger brothers. They fought and commanded in the founding days of Texas and the Mexican War. They were known for their bravery.

The Shely family had six brothers who were Rangers in the 1880s. This included Capt. Joe Shely of Company F.[7]

Tumlinson, Castro, White, Wright, Prince, Dean, Dendy, Hamer, and Allee are some of the families who have produced more than one Ranger.

The Allee Legacy

Alfred Y. Allee was the son and grandson of Texas Rangers. He was raised in the tradition. Born on a ranch in South Texas, Allee grew up in the area that he would later protect.

Captain Allee was one of the toughest Rangers of the mid-1900s. In 1969, his men helped contain an attempted jail break in Carrizo Springs.

As felons inside were shooting at officers, townspeople ducked for cover. Teargas shots failed to subdue the prisoners, so it was time to move. The criminals were on the second floor. The situation called for the Rangers to climb stairs while trying not to get shot.

When two of Allee's men started toward the steps, he pulled them back. "None of my Rangers are gonna get killed in front of me!" he said. Then the sixty-four-year-old captain took a machinegun, repositioned the cigar in his mouth, and charged up the stairs.

Bullets bounced around the walls and everyone else took cover. After a few thuds, the captain yelled down, "All clear!"[8]

That was the kind of Ranger Captain Allee was. He personified "one riot, one Ranger." Men who knew him and were cared for by his leadership would tell you he did everything for the state and the honor of the Texas Rangers. Captain Allee's son followed in his footsteps.

Many families have multiple Rangers in their heritage. Some families have only one Ranger but other law officers too. Law-enforcement families are close. Their service is often perpetuated generation to generation.

The Medal of Valor

The Texas Ranger is trustworthy, courageous, and dedicated. Some outstanding Rangers have earned the Texas DPS Commissioners' Medal of Valor, which is given "to officers who have displayed conspicuous gallantry, courage and heroism at considerable risk to their own lives." Four Texas Rangers have received this award: Sgt. William R. Gerth (1983), Sgt. Stanley Keith Guffey (1987, posthumously), Sgt. John Aycock (1987 and 1995), and Sgt. Danny V. Rhea (1998).

Each of these men chose to protect others even when faced with death. These Rangers showed great compassion for human life.

Ranger Johnnie Aycock is a courageous yet quiet and humble man. He is the only Ranger to have received the Medal of Valor twice. His first citation was for his work in the Kara-Leigh Whitehead kidnapping, and the second came after he saved a baby from a gunman.[9]

In the Line of Duty

Two Texas Rangers have been killed by criminals in the line of duty since 1935.

Ranger Bobby Doherty was killed during a marijuana "buy-bust" in 1978.

An informant led officers to a dealer in Denton County. During the raid and arrest, the dealer shot and killed Ranger Doherty.

Ranger Stan Guffey served with Company F. In 1987 he was killed while rescuing Kara-Leigh Whitehead from a kidnapper.[10] His efforts saved her life.

Each of these Texas Rangers gave up his life for his service. They did so for the people they saved and for the state. The potential for the ultimate sacrifice is always there. As for other law officers, it comes with the badge.

From saddle to cell phone, the end is still a good arrest.

Ranger H. Joaquin Jackson[11]

Chapter 13

Today's Texas Ranger

I treat people as nice as they will let me. I give them the choice. If you treat everyone with respect, you get respect.

Ranger Capt. Howard Duane "Dino" Henderson

Past and Present Prepare the Future

The Texas Rangers are a special investigative, crime-prevention, and law-enforcement agency of the Lone Star State. They uphold the laws of the state of Texas and the U.S. Constitution.[1] They seek the truth through evidence, wherever it is and however it turns out.

While these officers today are a new breed, they are made from solid and legendary stock. They now have different obstacles and amazing tools. Yet when it comes to their purpose of protection, these Rangers are doing the same job as in earlier times. The goal is to apprehend the criminal and defend the state. They preserve the peace.

Some of the modern Texas Rangers organization (Courtesy of the Texas Ranger Hall of Fame and Museum, Waco, TX)

Computer Crimes

Sometimes a crime is not bloody or even visible. An offender can invade a home through a computer. Crimes are now being committed on the Internet. There are scams to steal Texans' money or property and efforts to vandalize through computer viruses and communication crimes.[2] Some Internet criminals seek to harm children. These people are predators and thieves, and their crimes are real. Rangers investigate them too.

Criminals are using technology to do harm. They do not care about the damage they do. Rangers are working to make it harder for cyber-crooks to harm Texas.

A Constant in an Age of Change

Rangers have faced just about any villain imaginable. They have seen murderers, thieves, bank robbers, and hostile natives. Kidnappers, spies, out-of-control mobs, and corrupt politicians have opposed them. They have handled people blinded by racial hatred, aggressive strikers, feuding families, drug traffickers, gangsters, and more. Villains come and they go. Advances in technology are used to commit new crimes, and other technologies are used to solve them. The Texas constant in every case is the ready Ranger and his dedication.

As time passes, new officers come into the ranks. These Rangers now get extensive training, and the results are impressive even to a veteran. "The Ranger today—the skills and quality—amaze me," says Ranger Capt. Bob Bullock. "We send them to the training schools, like the one run by the University of Tennessee, with the body farm (UT Anthropology Research Facility) and all. They learn so much."[3] This training is now added to the original Texas Ranger savvy, work ethic, and integrity.

Today, a new Ranger usually starts as a Field Ranger. He handles assignments out of the office and gains experience in a variety of cases. He learns about Ranger duty and keeps practicing Ranger skills until they become instinct. The Field Ranger grows into a better officer through training, training, experience, and more training. Training continually prepares the law enforcer for future cases.

Part of the training involves getting used to the company. A new Ranger must become comfortable with those who have been there. It can be a bit overwhelming even after making it into the organization. "They are nervous that they might mess up," says Bullock. "I tell them, 'If you didn't screw something up, I'd be worried about you.'"[4] This demonstrates compassion with a sense of humor. It tells a newbie two things: he is okay, but do not mess up again.

The Heritage in Their Work

The Texas Rangers accomplish their job with love of the land, the West, and everything about the state. They honor the traditions of the horse, the weapon, the boots, the hat, and the star. However, now these officers are also cutting-edge crime-investigation professionals.[5] But even with all the newest equipment, the job still boils down to solving a crime puzzle.

"Sometimes you just can't figure it out, like a great big puzzle, and you don't have all the pieces," says Lt. George Turner, of Company F.

U.S. Marshals

The Rangers help when called. On occasion, this entails being authorized to suppress major disturbances in the state. Interagency cooperation and communication have always been there, but now, at times U.S. Marshals and Rangers are officially linked to reach a mutual goal.[6]

Since 2005, some Texas Rangers have been deputized as part of the U.S. Marshal Team. Those Rangers become a part of a Federal Task Force. They are sworn in as Special Deputy U.S. Marshals, which gives them jurisdiction wherever the task force may need them. The Texas Ranger can already cross county lines when necessary, but the task-force members have even more flexibility for special assignments.[7] Linking with the U.S. Marshals expands these Rangers' jurisdiction and helps bring fugitives to justice. This falls right in line with their regular dedication to public and private property.

Guardians Against Terrorism

Rangers are also involved in the battle against terrorism. The Rio Grande is approximately 1,900 miles long. Over 650 of those miles are in Texas. It is not just a long river but an international border. Terrorists from all parts of the world look for places to enter the U.S. The Texas-Mexico border is one of their targets.

Another possible point of entry is the Gulf Coast, which in Texas covers hundreds of miles. Huge refineries, cities, and military installations are sprinkled along this area. It is a tempting objective for America's enemies. As far back as Captain Burton's horse marines, the Texas Rangers have

2000-2023

TEXAS	UNITED STATES	THE WORLD
2000 Automatic shotguns standard Texas Ranger armament Phillips refinery explosion in Pasadena	**2001** September 11 Islamic terrorists attack New York City and the Pentagon; attack on White House failed	**2000** Gisborne, New Zealand is first city to enter the new millennium
	2004 Mars rovers land	
2005 The Texas Rangers can be deputized as part of a U.S. Marshals team	**2005** Hurricane Katrina hits the Gulf Coast	
2008 Hurricane Ike hits Galveston and Houston Raid on polygamist ranch		**2008** Chaiten volcano erupts in Chile Hadron Collider built in Geneva, Switzerland
2009 Fort Hood shooting	**2010** U.S. Census reports over 308,000,000 citizens	**2011** Osama Bin Laden killed
		2012 100th anniversary of *Titanic* sinking
2023 The Texas Rangers bicentennial	**2014** First cases of Ebola virus treated in U.S.	**2014** Malaysian Airlines Flight 370 disappears

guarded the coast. This continues today as a part of our nation's defense. Rangers work with federal and local agencies to protect against potential problems.

Crime and Entertainment

Crime-investigation movies and TV shows can make the Ranger's job harder. The real detective collects evidence and preserves it to catch lawbreakers. If a show exposes some of their investigational secrets, criminals can learn them also. Just as in the days of the republic, each side of the law is learning and improving its skills. The sharper the criminal becomes, the harder the Ranger has to work. The plain truth is that not all crimes get solved.

The Unsolved Crimes Investigation Team (UCIT) was initially a separate Ranger company, with its own lab and captain. In 2008, it was disbanded, and the highly qualified UCIT members moved into the other companies.

Solving these crimes requires tedious, time-consuming work. It is not filled with exciting activity, as is seen on TV. On the contrary, it demands patience, dedication, and hours of office paperwork. Rangers seek to resolve problems. They are on the case, hot or cold.

Weather Disasters

At times, weather is the enemy. From the Panhandle to the Rio Grande Valley, from west to east, Texas has all kinds of weather. There are harsh winters, hot summers, lack of water, and too much water. Forest fires and chemical accidents can occur. On the Gulf Coast, hurricanes create tremendous disorder. All these factors make missions difficult, but Rangers adapt. The job must be done. They have to expect the unexpected.

On September 13, 2008, Hurricane Ike hit the Gulf Coast. It crossed Galveston Island and followed the Houston Ship Channel northward into East Texas. Winds exceeded one hundred miles per hour, and tidal waters surged up to eighteen feet. By the time the storm passed, millions of people were without electricity and water. Some no longer had a home.

The Rangers were called in to assist the local law-enforcement agencies. Just as in hurricanes before, they were there to help wherever they were needed. One way they assisted was to increase the numbers of officers patrolling the affected areas.

Sgt. Ray G. Ramon, of Company D in Alice, Texas, was just one of the Rangers who left his usual territory to aid the hard-hit counties. He was assigned to lend a hand to the Galveston County Sheriff's Department in the coastal area of Kemah, Texas. "We were on standby a week before Ike hit," Ramon said. "We handed out MREs [Meals Ready to Eat] and [bottled] water while patrolling."[8] They were securing the peace and keeping an eye on property while aiding storm victims.

Texas Secret Service

The governor has his own protective detail. This is a secret-service patrol provided by the DPS. Sometimes this includes assistance from the Texas Rangers. As a part of the DPS, Rangers serve as the governor's security whenever necessary. This is especially true during official state travel and when other dignitaries come to visit.

It can also apply to other famous Texans. For example, former University of Texas football coach Mack Brown had Rangers nearby at an important game against Oklahoma. Danger comes in different forms.

Organized Crime

Crime organizations prey on citizens and property. To combat organized crime, peacekeepers get organized too.

The Texas Rangers battle all kinds of organized-crime elements. When gangs, drug cartels, and other criminal-interest groups break Texas laws, Rangers fight back in concert with other law-enforcement agencies.

Modern Criminals' Worst Nightmare

Today's criminal does not want today's Texas Ranger on his trail. If the Rangers are invited into a case—whether it be a murder, gang activity, or political corruption—that means someone called for expert help. Immediately, the Ranger investigator will gather information. He will question the local authorities and, if applicable, consult any federal agency involved. He will have a twenty-first-century forensic lab at his disposal. He will conduct computer work to gather all known data.

The officer will have cooperation from his and any other Ranger company. He will have the transportation he requires. This could be on an airline, observation plane, helicopter, or even a good horse. He also has access to the DPS tracking dogs.

Rangers make it a point to be well armed. The individual will have an arsenal unto himself. Each officer will have a minimum of main and backup side arms. Rangers must be qualified to use each and have them formally approved. Other necessities are a rifle and a shotgun. The Ranger will also be carrying handcuffs, leg irons, a transport belt, belt rig, and buckle. He will likely have plastic restraints (similar to giant zip ties). He will have a bulletproof vest and other body armor, a Kevlar helmet, a gasmask, and a riot baton. A raid jacket, coveralls, parka, BDUs (battle dress uniforms, or fatigues), and more will be at hand. This is all in addition to his standard, Western-style, lawman attire and "no messing around" steely stare.

To gather evidence, Rangers take along tools, such as laptops and other electronic devices, different types of cameras, a tripod, portable radio, portable printer, binoculars, flashlight, a Mela Beam Handheld Spotlight, fingerprint kit, evidence kit, bolt cutters, and other special technology. Properly collecting and documenting evidence is the goal.

Rangers also carry all sorts of special weapons and items individual to that officer. These are crime-fighting armaments, equipment for preparedness, and useful gadgets. Everything a Ranger carries is for a successful prosecution of a criminal.

The Non-Uniform

There is more to the Texas Ranger than boots, a hat, gun, and star. He does not have a set uniform. He can choose his way to dress in appropriate clothing. The Western white shirt, Western belt buckle, and boots are traditional and recognizable. So is the light-colored cowboy hat. Even though Rangers do not have an official uniform, it is not difficult to spot them. Essentially, they are always in uniform. They were it on the inside.

Transportation

If a Ranger does use a horse, his gear list increases. This includes horse trailers, especially for use in a full-scale mounted search.

Rangers are issued cars designed with enough engine power to catch the fast criminal. Each has an X900 radio, siren, and emergency red light. As a part of the DPS, Rangers also have access to reconnaissance planes, helicopters, assault tanks, and personnel carriers.

The key to all of these resources is the Ranger. He will have his badge for identification and department credit cards for funding what he still needs.

The Most Valuable Tools

Capt. Dino Henderson says that the Texas Ranger's pen is a valuable tool. That "pen is a piece of equipment that has put more people in jail" than most would believe. It takes notes, signs official papers, and expresses the Ranger's honesty and intellect.[9]

In the end, the sharpest, most necessary, and deadliest weapon the Texas Ranger carries is his mind. It is well prepared and has stored information from his formative years, college, and working life. It is his first connection with his commander and every assignment. It is the warehouse for his training and experience. It stores his moral integrity, dedication, and honor. It motivates actions and produces courage.

The Ranger today is prepared for every task. His knowledge helps him be a discerner of truth, logic, and justice. It is his duty to gather the facts that tell the whole story in order to solve cases. This function restores and keeps peace in Texas. The Texas Ranger does not make the laws, but he upholds them.

Captain Buckaloo is Texas real, as are the rest of his fellow Rangers. One look at him should make any criminal think seriously about going legit.

Charles Poland, referring to Clete Buckaloo[10]

Chapter 14
Honoring the Legacy

Every day of my Ranger career that badge compelled me to reach for the ideal.
Ranger H. Joaquin Jackson

The Badge

Law officials have worn badges since the time of the knights in Europe. They possessed insignia from the king or nobleman whom they represented. However, the Rangers did not have badges until after the Civil War. By the 1870s, it became clear that the Frontier Battalion and Special Force needed to have their authority recognized. A group of mounted men riding up to a ranch could be Rangers or someone quite different. Identification was needed. However, what the Ranger received was not a badge. It was a piece of paper.

The Warrant of Authority was a document from the Texas Adjutant General's Office. The Ranger would fold it up and keep it in his pocket. Then when he needed to prove he was a law official, he could.

Official badge use started with the DPS. Before that time, badges were made to each Ranger's specifications. Legend says that Texas Rangers sat around the campfire and carved out star badges from a Mexican cinco-peso coin. That would take a lot of carving. Badges *could* be made out of the Mexican coins in the past, if a Ranger wanted that. An expert jeweler, gunsmith, or specialist craftsman would have to make it. Some Rangers had homemade badges as early as the late 1800s through the 1920s.[1]

The official badge is believed to have been patterned after the first seal of Texas. This was not the state seal but the one created at the first convention of Texians (1835). The seal was made from a star-shaped pearl button. It proclaimed the Texians' intent to have independence from Mexico. The makeshift seal became a symbol to the Texan forefathers, some of whom were Rangers.

The button belonged to the secretary of the convention, Charles Stewart. He described the shape on the seal as "a fitting emblem of a new star arisen—in the galaxy of states."[2]

At the turn of the twentieth century, there were also shield-shaped badges. These were not usually worn by the regular Ranger. Instead, someone like a Special Railroad Ranger (paid by the railroad) would have these.

When the DPS took command, badges became part of the standard Ranger attire. The first was shaped like a shield. In 1957, the badge was round and spelled out *T-E-X-A-S* on a solid blue field. These were nicknamed "bottle cap" badges.

In 1962, the badge changed again. Since then, the Rangers have worn the star-and-wagon-wheel badge. The exact design changes a bit from time to time, but the symbols, from the state seal of Texas, remain the same.

Today the badge is a standard issue and it is uniform. The present-day Texas Ranger badge is distinctive. It is silver with a five-pointed star in the center of a wagon-wheel circle. The circle has an oak branch on one side and olive branch on the other. The branches stand for strength and peace. The words *Dept. of Public Safety* are at the top and *Texas Rangers* at the bottom.

When a Texas Ranger first pins on that badge, his life has taken a turn. After twenty-nine years of service, Ranger Barry Caver put it this way: "A lot of respect and responsibility come with it and it's instantaneous the day you pin it on."[3] That badge stands for something. The officer bears the responsibility to earn the respect.

The Texas Ranger Hall of Fame and Museum

In 1967, construction began on a log and stone building in Waco, Texas. This would become the home of Texas Ranger memories and history. The Texas Ranger Hall of Fame and Museum (TRHFM) architecture and location perfectly capture both the tough beginnings of the organization as well as its fast road to the future.

When visitors go to the TRHFM, they are greeted by two statues. One is a mounted figure of a Western minuteman, flag in hand, ready to protect. The other sculpture is of Ranger George B. Erath. They silently give testimony to the Old West and all the adventure that Texas has seen.

Inside the museum, numerous rooms are filled with displays from before 1823 to the present. This includes a detailed research library and vast history files. Equipment, weapons, badges, and photos pack the walls. It is a place of special honor and legacy. The museum gives a close view of the unique Texas Ranger history.

Guardians of Honor

Part of Texas Ranger duty is to handle the inquiries into suspected misconduct among the ranks of the Texas DPS or government representatives. They have investigated crime since the beginning, but now they pursue lawbreakers even if they are government officials or peace officers. Those who are sworn to protect and serve are not above the law. The Texas Rangers are there to make sure.

Invisible Hero

Most of the time, the public and criminals do not even know Rangers are around. They apply their equipment and techniques without fanfare. The media will occasionally mention Ranger involvement, but they only see the surface. Rangers are always exploring offenses, behind the scenes. Then they share information with other law enforcement. When a case comes to a close, they may not and do not need to get credit. Credit is not the goal.

For the Ranger, that is not a problem. They know who did what, and the completion of the task is its own glory. "The end result is what counts," says Ranger Lt. Jeff Collins of Company C.

To Become a Texas Ranger

To accomplish the goal of becoming one of the Texas Ranger peacekeeping ranks, the applicant must meet the standards. The standards are high. Those who want to be Rangers need to make the right choices at a young age. "You can't let your life get in the way of your Texas Ranger duty," says Capt. Alvin A. Alexis II.[4]

Applicants must meet a number of criteria to be considered. There is a test, and the highest-scoring selected candidates are then required to appear before the Oral Interview Board. After the interviews, new Rangers are chosen from the top scores and only enough to fill openings in the ranks. If no Ranger hopeful meets the standard, the spot stays vacant until the next year's selection.

Even if an applicant does everything right, sometimes there is no opening. The only thing to do then is go home and perhaps try again next year. Many Texas Rangers applied more than once.

When the new Rangers are selected, they are approved and assigned to a company. Capt. Dino Henderson says, "We want someone who isn't afraid to work and goes beyond the call of duty."

The state legislature sets the number of Rangers allowed. Today, the maximum number of commissioned Texas Rangers, in service at one time, is 150.

Ranger Companies

There are several Texas Ranger companies (field operations units). They cover the state and are grouped for service. Headquarters is located in Austin, Texas.

The companies are identified by letters. Company A is usually on the east side of the state, headquartered in Houston, Texas. The others are identified in like manner but subject to change.

Each company covers vast areas and populations. They have particular assignments, duties, and expertise. The border companies especially have this, since they are on an international border and their responsibilities include national security. The border between Mexico and the U.S. includes twenty-one crossings. Still, the Texas Rangers are a state organization. Cooperation with the U.S. government takes place under the direction of the government of Texas.

Special Teams

The Texas Rangers have special operations commanders and duties. They handle Special Weapons and Tactics (SWAT), Ranger Reconnaissance, the Crisis Negotiation Team (CNT), Bomb Squad or Explosive Ordnance Disposal, Border Security Operations Center (BSOC), Joint Operations and Intelligence Center (JOIC), and Special Response Teams (SRTs). The Texas Legislature has allowed UCIT and Public Corruption divisions also. These units and their captains oversee the process and strategy of the team operations.

Cooperation and Success

In 1968, murder occurred in Big Spring, Texas. A dog-kennel owner had been shot, right in front of his son. From that point on, several law-enforcement organizations worked together to solve the case. Through teamwork, they brought the murderers to justice.

The Ranger assigned to the investigation was E. G. "Butch" Albers, Jr. Before the guilty had their day in court, he worked with the Big Spring Police Department, Howard County Sheriff's Office, Kansas City (Missouri)

Police Vice Squad, and Midland office of the DPS. Three suspects were convicted. Ranger Albers was found to be patient, diligent, and "one of the best interrogators" Kansas City Police Detective James Theisen had ever seen.[5]

"It's all about cooperation and communication," says Captain Henderson. "And in the Texas Rangers, this is superior." Communication is part of the game, and the Rangers are good at it. Law enforcement depends on teamwork.

Captain Henderson says, "I read books, probably in elementary and junior high, about Ranger lore, and I was always fascinated with the West." Western films also attracted him. "They always got their man, especially the John Wayne [movies]. Seeing John Wayne on the screen and what I learned to do as the right thing was an influence for real life."

To become a success as a Texas Ranger, Captain Henderson took parts of the books and movies that he experienced as a young person, used the training his family and schools gave him, and applied real-life lessons from his law-enforcement years. He learned what it meant to be a clear-thinking adult, a leader, a Ranger. "Your reputation is who other people think you are. Your character is who you actually are. The goal is to make them match."

He says being a Ranger is an honor and it is a person-to-person job.

Today's One Ranger

In homes, neighborhoods, and cities today, the early Texas Ranger may seem farfetched. There are different forms of transportation now, and some people have never seen a horse up close. Most Texans live in dense communities or huge cities. The ranch or farm, while still with us, is no longer every Texan's home. Dangers and attackers are different, but unfortunately they still exist.

When Rangers are on the trail of a lawbreaker, their training and experience kick in automatically. Learning from successes and mistakes, Rangers move forward with the same indomitable character as the pioneer lawmen. Working as a team, they provide assistance with new technologies and age-old courage.

Daily defense is essential in all states. Police, state troopers, the military branches, sheriffs, firemen, and the government are there to serve the people. In Texas, the Rangers are a unique part of that protection. They are proficient in using all their gear, and their duty is to the state. The Rangers' dedication is the same as it has always been. They are ready.

Whether it is one Ranger or the whole force, a Texas Ranger is there. They pursue murderers, robbers, attackers, and conmen. They investigate credit-card, computer, and counterfeit crimes.

Over the almost two hundred years of Texas Ranger history, between ten and twelve thousand Rangers have served. The numbers are inexact because early records are incomplete.[6]

Rangers do a job, do it well, and then move on. When local authorities were not able to maintain control, Rangers were there to lend a lawful hand.

The legacy of the starred badge is about the independent Texas spirit and the dedication to keep it that way. However, from the beginning, Texans were people who became a part of something bigger than themselves. For the benefit of their state, Texas Rangers take a bit of their independent spirit and donate it to something bigger again. They give it to the preservation of their state. They have never been concerned about whether the odds are stacked against them. What matters is that they work to make things right.

The Ranger legacy is following orders and thinking under pressure. It is being ready to serve when help is requested. It is independence from peer pressure or personal credit. It is guarding this state's citizens and property, no matter the odds. It is honoring the Lone Star by keeping order in a courtroom, polling place, campus, or bar. It is being a careful evidence collector and truthful witness so justice may be given.

Each situation is different, but the legacy is the same. Each Ranger is prepared to be a defender and a law enforcer. He protects the state and U.S. laws.

Like strong spokes in the wagon wheel of their badge, each does the work necessary for the wheel to keep functioning. The Rangers work as a united whole. The Texas Rangers organization is itself the Lone Star legacy.

They were men who could not be stampeded.

Col. Homer Garrison, DPS director[7]

Notes

Chapter 1

1. H. Joaquin Jackson and David Marion Wilkinson, *One Ranger: A Memoir* (Austin: University of Texas Press, 2005), 38.

2. Ibid.

3. "Texas Ranger History: Timeline—Defending the Law," Texas Ranger Hall of Fame and Museum, 2008, http://www.texasranger.org/history/Timedefend.htm.

4. Charles H. Harris III and Louis R. Sadler, *The Texas Rangers and the Mexican Revolution: The Bloodiest Decade, 1910-1920* (Albuquerque: University of New Mexico Press, 2004), 1.

5. Mike Cox, "A Brief History of the Texas Rangers," Texas Ranger Hall of Fame and Museum, October 1, 2008, http://www.texasranger.org/history/BriefHistory1.htm.

6. R. B. Thieme, Jr., *Freedom Through Military Victory* (Houston: R. B. Thieme, Jr., Bible Ministries, 1996), dedication.

7. Charles M. Robinson III, *The Men Who Wear the Star: The Story of the Texas Rangers* (New York: Random House, 2000), 248.

8. Cox.

9. "The Best of the Real West: The Texas Rangers"(New York: A&E Television Networks, 2000), DVD.

Chapter 2

1. June 10, 2008, http://www.50states.com/facts/texas.htm.

2. Robinson.

3. Nina Romberg, phone call to author, 2008.

4. Frederick Wilkins, *The Legend Begins: The Texas Rangers, 1823-1845* (Austin: State House Press, 1996), 3.

5. "Texas State Historical Association Texas Almanac: American Indians in Texas," January 2015, http://www.texasalmanac.com/topics/culture/american-indian/american-indian.

6. Walter Prescott Webb, *Texas Rangers: A Century of Frontier Defense*, 18th ed. (1935; repr., Austin: University of Texas Press, 2005), 21.

7. "The Best of the Real West."

8. Webb, 20.

9. Texas Ranger Hall of Fame and Museum, January 2008, http://www.texasranger.org/history/BriefHistory1.htm.

10. Ibid.
11. Ibid.

Chapter 3

1. Texas Ranger Hall of Fame and Museum, http://www.texasranger.org/history/BriefHistory1.htm.
2. Webb, 23.
3. Ibid.
4. "Robert McAlpin Williamson," Texas State Cemetery, February 2008, http://www.cemetery.state.tx.us/pub/user_form822.asp?pers_id=50.
5. Webb, 38-39.
6. Robinson, 38.
7. Webb, 27.

Chapter 4

1. Stephen L. Moore, *Savage Frontier*, vol. 2, *1838-1839* (Denton: University of North Texas Press, 2006), ix.
2. "Comancheria: Rise of the Comanche," World Historia International Community, January 2015, http://www.worldhistoria.com/comancheria-the-rise-of-the-comanches_topic127991.html.
3. Wilkins, 78.
4. Ibid., 79; Webb, 55-57.
5. Webb, 63.
6. Ibid., 59.
7. Wilkins, 54, 83.
8. Webb, 82.
9. Christy Smith (research librarian, Armstrong Texas Ranger Research Center, Texas Ranger Hall of Fame and Museum) and Christina Stopka (deputy director, Armstrong Texas Ranger Research Center, Texas Ranger Hall of Fame and Museum), in discussion with the author, October 2008.
10. Moore, 356.
11. Wilkins, 167.
12. "The Best of the Real West."
13. Wilkins, 63.
14. Ibid., 181.
15. Ibid., 181.
16. Ibid., 178-82.
17. "The Best of the Real West."

Chapter 5

1. "Texas Ranger History: The Ranging Tradition 1821-1836," Texas Ranger Hall of Fame and Museum, January 9, 2007, http://www.texasranger.org/history/Timeranging.htm.

2. Moore, 356.
3. Steve Moore, "Ranger Mathew Old Paint Caldwell," Summer 2003, http://texasranger.org/dispatch/Backissues/Dispatch_Issue_11.pdf.
4. Wilkins, 128-35.
5. Webb, 74.
6. Ibid., 77.
7. Robinson, 68-69.
8. "The Best of the Real West."

Chapter 6

1. Webb, 119-20.
2. Robinson, 76.
3. Webb, 113.
4. "The Best of the Real West."
5. Webb, 12-24.
6. Ibid., 138-39.
7. Moore, *Savage Frontier,* 357.
8. Robinson, 108.
9. Webb, 124.
10. Ibid., 239.
11. "Who Was Sul Ross?" Sul Ross State University, 2015, http://www.sulross.edu/page/1065/lawrence-sullivan-ross.
12. James T. DeShields, *Cynthia Ann Parker: The Story of Her Capture* (San Antonio: Naylor, 1934).
13. "Texas Ranger History: Timeline—Defending the Law."
14. Robinson, 155.
15. Webb, 219.
16. Ibid.
17. Ibid., 219-20.
18. Ibid., 231.

Chapter 7

1. Webb, 309.
2. Ibid., 233.
3. Robinson, 169.
4. Webb, 233.
5. "The Best of the Real West."
6. Ibid.
7. Webb, 288.
8. Ibid., 299-300.
9. Ibid., 371.
10. Ibid., 328.
11. "The Best of the Real West."

Chapter 8

1. Webb, 457.

2. Casey Edward Greene and Shelly Henley Kelly, eds., *Through a Night of Horrors* (College Station: Texas A & M University Press, 2000), 3.

3. Webb, 463.

4. Ibid., 466-69.

5. Harris, epigraph.

6. Robinson, 282.

7. Harris, 532.

8. Webb, 517.

9. Robert M. Utley, *Lone Star Lawmen* (New York: Oxford University Press, 2007), 115.

10. "Marvin 'Red' Burton 1885-1970," Texas Ranger Hall of Fame—State Designated Memorial, October 22, 2008, http://www.texasranger.org/halloffame/Burton_Marvin.htm.

11. Utley, 122.

12. Webb, 455.

Chapter 9

1. Brownson Malsch, *"Lone Wolf" Gonzaullas, Texas Ranger*, rev. ed. (Norman: University of Oklahoma Press, 1998), 37.

2. Ibid., 17-20.

3. Harris, 2.

4. Utley, 136.

5. Ibid., 124.

Chapter 10

1. Utley, 194.

2. Ibid., 196.

3. Ibid., 125.

4. "Texas Ranger History: Timeline—Special," Texas Ranger Hall of Fame and Museum, January 31, 2015, http://www.texasranger.org/history/Timespecial.htm.

5. Lt. George Turner, in discussion with the author, March 2008.

6. Utley, 94.

7. "James 'Jim' Riddles 1910-1975," Texas Ranger Hall of Fame—State Designated Memorial, February 2015, http://www.texasranger.org/halloffame/Riddles_James.htm.

8. Utley, 204-5.

9. Ibid., 218-19.

10. Ibid., 220.

11. Ibid., 223.

12. Ibid., 240.

13. Ibid., 243.

14. Ibid., 242-43, 246.
15. Ibid., 220.

Chapter 11

1. Jackson and Wilkinson, 63-65.
2. Utley, 296.
3. Ibid., 295-96.
4. Ibid., 296.
5. Jackson and Wilkinson, 183.
6. Utley, 304-6.
7. Courtney Barry, "DPS Rangers: A History in the Making," *Texas Highway Patrol Magazine* 13, no. 2 (Summer 2008): 8.
8. Utley, 307.
9. Utley, 323-24.
10. "The Rafael Resendez-Ramirez Case: A Review of the INS's Actions and the Operation of its IDENT Automated Fingerprint Identification System," USDOJ/OIG Special Report, September 19, 2008, http://www.usdoj.gov/oig/special/0003/index.htm.
11. Jeff Cook (Company A Ranger), in discussion with the author, April 2007.
12. "Silver Stars and Sixguns," Texas Department of Public Safety, January 2015, http://www.txdps.state.tx.us/TexasRangers/silverstars.htm.

Chapter 12

1. Moore, *Savage Frontier,* 69, 272.
2. Stopka.
3. Rebekkah Lohr (librarian), in discussion with the author, April 2008.
4. "The Best of the Real West."
5. Wilkins, 37.
6. Harris, 42, 234.
7. Ibid., 22.
8. Jackson and Wilkinson, 153.
9. Ibid., 184; "The DPS Medal of Honor," Texas Department of Public Safety, January 2015, http://dps.texas.gov/medalofvalor.htm.
10. Jackson and Wilkinson, 184.
11. Ibid., 42.

Chapter 13

1. Cook.
2. Barry, 9.
3. "The Body Farm," *UTNE Reader,* October 23, 2008, http://www.utne.com/1999-05-01/the-body-farm.aspx.
4. Capt. Bob Bullock (Company E Ranger), in discussion with the author, October 2008.

5. Utley, 330.

6. "United States Marshals Swears in the Texas Rangers as Special Deputy United States Marshals," *Museum News & Events*, September 1, 2008, http://www.texasranger.org/news/new/htm; Lt. Jeff Collins (Company C Ranger), in discussion with the author, October 2008.

7. "Texas Rangers: Job Duties," Texas Department of Public Safety, January 2008, http://www.txdps.state.tx.us/director_staff/texas_rangers/.

8. Sgt. Ray G. Ramon, in discussion with the author, October 2008.

9. Capt. Howard Duane "Dino" Henderson, in discussion with the author, March 2008.

10. Pamela Colloff, "Roar of the Crowd," *Texas Monthly* (June 2007).

Chapter 14

1. "Ranger History: Historic Badges of the Texas Rangers," Texas Ranger Hall of Fame and Museum, 2015, http://www.texasranger.org/history/HistoricBadges.htm.

2. Ibid.

3. "Ranger Captain Reflects on Waco, Fort Davis," *Midland Reporter-Telegram*, February 2015, http://www.mrt.com/news/top_stories/article_b047925e-1749-51da-81de-db1b5e2d665f.html?mode=story.

4. Capt. Alvin A. Alexis II, in discussion with the author, June 2010.

5. E. G. Albers, Jr., *The Life and Reflections of a Texas Ranger* (Waco: Texian Press, 1998), 69-75.

6. Rachel Barnett (research librarian, Texas Ranger Hall of Fame and Museum), in discussion with the author, March 2008.

7. Utley, 196.

Bibliography

Books

Albers, E. G., Jr. *The Life and Reflections of a Texas Ranger.* Waco: Texian Press, 1998.

Cox, Mike. *The Texas Rangers: Men of Action & Valor.* Austin: Eakin Press, 1991.

DeShields, James T. *Cynthia Ann Parker: The Story of Her Capture.* San Antonio: Naylor, 1934.

Dobie, J. Frank. *Mustangs.* Lincoln: University of Nebraska Press, 2005.

Greene, Casey Edward, ed. *Through a Night of Horrors.* College Station: Texas A & M University Press, 2000.

Harris, Charles H., III, and Louis R. Sadler. *The Texas Rangers and the Mexican Revolution: The Bloodiest Decade, 1910-1920.* Albuquerque: University of New Mexico Press, 2004.

Haynes, Sam W. *Soldiers of Misfortune: The Somervell and Mier Expeditions.* Austin: University of Texas Press, 1990.

Jackson, H. Joaquin, and David Marion Wilkinson. *One Ranger: A Memoir.* Austin: University of Texas Press, 2005.

Knowles, Thomas W. *They Rode for the Lone Star: The Saga of the Texas Rangers.* 2nd ed. Bryan, TX: Lone Star, 2009.

Malsch, Brownson. *"Lone Wolf" Gonzaullas, Texas Ranger.* Rev. ed. Norman: University of Oklahoma Press, 1998.

Miller, John Morris, and A. T. Miller. *A Private in the Texas Rangers: A. T. Miller of Company B, Frontier Battalion.* Canseco-Keck History Series 3. College Station: Texas A & M Press, 2001.

Moore, Stephen L. *Savage Frontier.* Vol. 2, *1838-1839.* Denton: University of North Texas Press, 2006.

Newcomb, W. W., Jr. *The Indians of Texas.* Austin: University of Texas Press, 1972.

Paine, Albert Bigelow. *Captain Bill McDonald, Texas Ranger; a Story of Frontier Reform.* Whitefish, MT: Kessinger, 2005.

Proctor, Ben. *Just One Riot.* Austin: Eakin Press, 2000.

Robinson, Charles M., III. *The Men Who Wear the Star: The Story of the Texas Rangers.* New York: Random House, 2000.

Sterling, William Warren. *Trails & Trials of a Texas Ranger.* Norman: University of Oklahoma Press, 1968.

Thieme, R. B., Jr. *Freedom Through Military Victory.* Houston: R. B. Thieme, Jr., Bible Ministries, 1996.

Tuchman, Barbara W. *The Zimmermann Telegram.* New York: Ballantine Books, 1966.

Utley, Robert M. *Lone Star Lawmen.* New York: Oxford University Press, 2007.

Webb, Walter Prescott. *Texas Rangers: A Century of Frontier Defense.* 18th ed. Austin: University of Texas Press, 2005. First published 1935 by Houghton Mifflin.

Wilkins, Frederick. *Defending the Borders: The Texas Rangers, 1848-1861.* Austin: State House Press, 2001.

——. *The Legend Begins: The Texas Rangers, 1823-1845.* Austin: State House Press, 1996.

Periodicals

Barry, Courtney. "DPS Rangers: A History in the Making." *Texas Highway Patrol Magazine* 13, no. 2 (Summer 2008).

Colloff, Pamela. "Roar of the Crowd." *Texas Monthly* (June 2007): 119.

"One Riot; One Ranger: The Texas Ranger Hall of Fame and Museum." *Heart of Texas Electric Cooperative Magazine.* http://www.texasranger.org/news/HOT_Electric_Coop_2-09.pdf.

Rogers, Patrick. "The Man in the White Hat." *People* 2, no. 6 (August 16, 1999).

Texas Ranger Hall of Fame and Museum Visitors Guide.

The Texas Rangers: A History Map! Norman, OK: Map Ink, 1996.

Interviews

Texas Ranger Capt. Alvin A. Alexis II, Company D. June 21, 2010.

Rachel Barnett, research librarian, Texas Ranger Hall of Fame and Museum, March 25, 2008.

Bob Bowen, Stephen F. Austin University, 2008.

Texas Ranger Capt. Clete Buckaloo, headquarters. July 2 and 19, 2010.

Texas Ranger Capt. Bob Bullock, headquarters. October 3, 2008, and 2010.

Texas Ranger Lt. Jeff Collins, Company C. October 3, 2008.

Texas Ranger Sgt. Jeff Cook, Company A. April 25, 2007.

Texas Ranger Joe Haralson, Company A. July 5, 2010.

Texas Ranger Capt. Howard Duane "Dino" Henderson, headquarters. March 2008.

Dr. W. Karn, former physician in the Texas Department of Corrections. October 19, 2008.

Texas Ranger Lt. Brooks Long, Company E. June 24, 2010.

Texas Ranger Frank J. Malinak, Company F. June 15, 2010.

Cynthia Leal Massey, author.

Texas Ranger Capt. Shawn Palmer, Company G. June 25, 2010.

Texas Ranger Ronald Pettigrew, Company B. June 14, 2010.

Texas Ranger Sgt. Ray G. Ramon, Company D. October 3, 2008.

Craig Reinhold, former U.S. Army Ranger.

Texas Ranger Capt. Jeffery Robertson, headquarters. July 1, 2010.

Nina Romberg, author.

Christy Smith, research librarian, Armstrong Texas Ranger Research Center, Texas Ranger Hall of Fame and Museum, October 3, 2008.

Christina Stopka, deputy director, Armstrong Texas Ranger Research Center, Texas Ranger Hall of Fame and Museum, March, July, and October 2008; April

and July 2010; January 2015.
Christine Taylor-Butler, author.
Texas Ranger Lt. George Turner, Company F. March 25, 2008.
Jason Walker, director of research, Texas State Cemetery.

Museums and Historical Sites Visited

Bullock Texas State History Museum, Austin, Texas.
Company A, Richardson Ranger office, Richardson, Texas.
Lockhart State Park, Texas.
Texas Ranger Hall of Fame and Museum, Waco, Texas.
Texas Ranger Headquarters, Austin, Texas.
Texas State Cemetery, Austin, Texas.

Videos

Nonfiction

"The Best of the Real West: The Texas Rangers." DVD. New York: A&E Television Networks, 2000.

Fiction

The Alamo. Starring John Wayne, Richard Widmark, and Laurence Harvey.
The Comancheros. Starring John Wayne and Stuart Whitman, costarring Lee Marvin.
The Searchers. Directed by John Ford, starring John Wayne, costarring Natalie Wood.
Walker, Texas Ranger. Starring Chuck Norris.

Selected Web Sites

Geography and Statistics

"Texas Fast Facts." Accessed June 10, 2008. http://www.50states.com/facts/texas.htm.

History

"1993: Waco Cult Siege Ends in Inferno." Accessed April 7, 2010. http://news.bbc.co.uk/onthisday/hi/dates/stories/april/19/newsid_2489000/2489769.stm.
Texas State Historical Association Online. "Permanent Council." Handbook of Texas. Accessed July 17, 2010. http://www.tshaonline.org/handbook/online/articles/PP/ngp1.html.

American Indians

Moore, R. E. *The Alabama-Coushatta Indians*. Accessed October 17, 2008. http://www.texasindians.com/albam.htm.

Lone Ranger

Shayt, David H. *Hi-Yo, Silver! Away!* Accessed July 16, 2010. http://www.smithsonianmag.com/history-archaeology/Hi-Yo_Silver_Away.html?c=y&page=1.

Maps

Texas A&M University. "Coahuila y Tejas, 1836 Southeast Sector." Accessed July 18, 2010. http://www.tamu.edu/ccbn/dewitt/co&texse.htm.

Texas Department of Public Safety

"Department of Public Safety: Activity Summary." Accessed July 23, 2010. http://www.txdps.state.tx.us/TexasRangers/activitysummary.htm.

Texas Ranger Hall of Fame and Museum. "Commissioners' Medal of Valor Citations: Texas Rangers." Accessed August 1, 2010. http://www.texasranger.org/today/medalvalor.htm.

Texas Ranger History

Cox, Mike. *Texas Ranger Hall of Fame and Museum: A Brief History of Texas Rangers.* Accessed July 18, 2010. http://www.texasranger.org/history/BriefHistory1.htm.

Texas Rangers

Texas Ranger Hall of Fame and Museum. "Bob Crowder." Accessed June 1, 2010. http://www.texasranger.org/halloffame/Crowder_Bob.htm.

Texas Rangers Today

Cawthon, Ranger Matt, and Capt. Clete Buckaloo. *Standard Issue Field Equipment.* Accessed July 1, 2010. http://www.texasranger.org/today/Equipment.htm.

Index